AWAKEN THE
POWER
OF
FAITH

When you can See, there is no need to Believe

AWAKEN THE
POWER OF FAITH

When you can See, there is no need to Believe

S I R S H R E E
Author of the bestseller *The Source*

Awaken The Power Of Faith
When you can See, there is no need to Believe
By Sirshree Tejparkhi

Copyright © Tejgyan Global Foundation
All Rights Reserved 2019

Tejgyan Global Foundation is a charitable organization
with its headquarters in Pune, India.

ISBN : 978-93-87696-92-1

Published by WOW Publishings Pvt. Ltd., India

First edition published in July 2019

Second reprint published in February 2025

Printed and bound by Trinity Academy For Corporate Training Ltd, Pune

Based on the Hindi book titled 'Vishwas Niyam' by Sirshree Tejparkhi

Copyright and publishing rights are vested exclusively with WOW Publishings Pvt. Ltd. This book is sold subject to the condition that it shall not by way of trade or otherwise, be lent, resold, hired out, or otherwise circulated without the publisher's prior written consent in any form of binding or cover other than that in which it is published and without a similar condition including this condition being imposed on the subsequent purchaser and without limiting the rights under copyright reserved above, no part of this publication may be reproduced, stored in or introduced into a retrieval system, or transmitted, in any form, or by any means, electronic, mechanical, photocopying, recording or otherwise, without the prior written permission of both the copyright owner and the above-mentioned publisher of this book. Any person who does any unauthorized act in relation to this publication may be liable to criminal prosecution and civil claims for damages.
Although the author and publisher have made every effort to ensure accuracy of content in this book, they hereby disclaim any liability to any party for any loss, damage, or disruption caused by errors or omissions, resulting from negligence, accident, or any other cause. Readers are advised to take full responsibility to exercise discretion in understanding and applying the content of this book.

*To those who are physically challenged,
and yet place unflinching faith
in the benevolence of life;
To those who do not have eyesight,
but have the eyes of faith.*

Contents

		Preface	9
	Part I	**The Context Of Faith And Beliefs**	**13**
1		Faith And Beliefs	15
2		Everything Is A Game Of Beliefs	23
	Part II	**Principles Of Faith**	**31**
3	Principle 1	The Faith Frame	33
4	Principle 2	The Seed Of Faith	41
5		Catalyst To Manifest The Seed Of Faith	52
6	Principle 3	Life Is On Autopilot	66
7	Principle 4	The Highest Form Of Faith	79
8		The Voice Of Faith	85
9	Principle 5	Betrayal Is A Myth, Faith The Truth	94
10	Principle 6	Transformation With 100 % Faith	105
11	Principle 7	The Ultimate Evolved State Of Faith	113
	Part III	**Beyond Faith**	**121**
12		Transcendence Of Faith	123
13		Starting From The Finishing Line	131
14		The State Beyond Faith	138
	Appendix 1	The Journey Of Faith	143
	Appendix 2	Faith, Hope And Confidence	149
	Appendix 3	Principles Of Faith - Quick Reference	157

Preface

"As within, so without; as above, so below."

This maxim, which constitutes the Hermetic principles, truly encompasses the secret of the way life works. It sums up the fundamental law of life – our experience of the outside world is a reflection of our inner world. Our inner world is made of thoughts and feelings, which are based on the beliefs that we harbor. And our beliefs are empowered by our faith.

Let us consider the nature of faith with the help of an example.

> One pleasant morning, a man was strolling in a garden, lost in the concerns of his life situations. He saw a man playing with his little child. The father would toss his child up in the air and grab her when she came down. The little girl was utterly enjoying this game. Higher the father tossed her, the louder she would laugh and giggle!
>
> The man kept looking at this wondrous scene for a while and got a thought – What faith does the girl have on her father! She is not worried whether she would fall or get hurt after being tossed so high.
>
> The man further considered how he would have felt if he were to be tossed up that way. He would be extremely scared and terrified

about whether he would fall down. The little girl, however, had no such qualms. She was completely relaxed and was thoroughly enjoying the experience. How could she be so assured!

Finally, the man smiled. He had discovered the solution to his worries. Unflinching faith! Surrender! The little girl had unflinching faith on her father. She could naturally surrender and experience the joy of the present moment, without a thought about the future.

Can we have the same faith in God, in Nature, in the Higher power (whatever you may call it)? When Nature sends us a problem, it has already arranged for its solution, just as the father, who tosses his child up, safely holds her when she comes down. We just need to place faith.

This understanding of how faith works in our lives can bring about a paradigm shift in our perspective towards life. It can help us harness the power of faith to attain the ultimate purpose of life and realize our fullest potential.

Faith is the greatest vibration in the universe. It is the most potent power that we are blessed with. Ironically, it remains unexpressed or partly expressed in most peoples' lives. It is only when we fully unleash faith that we can experience true contentment.

By design, faith is inherent within us since our birth. It does not have to be acquired from outside. This is why we see children instinctively expressing faith. As children, it was very easy and natural for us to place faith in those around us. We did not have to be taught this. It is for this very reason that the little girl has undeterred faith when her father tosses her up. She has the deep assurance that the same hands that have tossed her up will also hold her.

The human mind gets conditioned with upbringing, due to which faith begins to wane with age. As we grow up, feelings of insecurity and distrust can take root in our psyche in response to testing incidents and challenging situations. Such feelings shroud our faith to a great extent, and sometimes completely.

Incidents like failure or betrayal make us sceptics. We stop trusting people fully; we lose faith in ourselves and begin to live with a victim mindset. This can become a deeply ingrained pattern, causing discontent, resentment and fear in the lives of many people.

This book throws light on what faith truly is, how the magic of faith works in our lives, how it gets shrouded and how it can be awakened and harnessed.

It further describes the ultimate evolved state of faith, where we realize who-we-truly-are, beyond the temporary, beyond our persona. When we realize our essence and get established in our true nature, we discover that we need not place faith in anything, simply because we become one with it. We realize that we *are* faith itself. We go beyond the need to believe, because we know!

The book comprises three parts –

Part I – The Context of Faith and Beliefs, introduces the context and relevance of faith. It explains the role that beliefs play in our lives and how faith relates to beliefs. With examples from everyday life, we will see how our beliefs can impact our physical health, social harmony, financial and emotional wellbeing.

Part II – Principles of Faith, discusses the 7 principles with which we can guide our lives, so as to align ourselves with the highest vibration in the universe. The Power of Faith has a bearing on all of creation. It determines how life unfolds.

Each principle is complete in itself and addresses a unique aspect of faith. It is important to contemplate these principles to find how they apply in your life. It is only through contemplation that you can translate these principles into practice in everyday life.

Principle 1 explains how faith can be raised in order to change the results of your actions.

Principle 2 deals with how nature responds to your faith and manifests things in your life.

Principle 3 helps in gaining a deep assurance in the providence of life and getting rid of anxiety.

Principle 4 explains the highest form of faith and how it can be awakened within you.

Principle 5 helps in overcoming hurtful feelings that arise from betrayal or failure and reinforcing trust in life.

Principle 6 explains the roadblocks in the journey of raising faith and how faith leads to transformation.

Principle 7 deals with how the pinnacle of faith – divine faith – works in life.

Part III – Beyond Faith, discusses the blossoming of life beyond divine faith. When one reaches the culmination of the journey in the evolution of faith, one transcends it. Life operates from the absolute, changeless and limitless standpoint of the true Self.

Appendix I explains the 7 kinds of faith that are essential to realize the true purpose of our lives.

Appendix II provides answers to questions raised by seekers of Truth on Faith, Superstitions, Hope and Confidence.

To make the most of this book, read it with faith – even if a little. It is more important to contemplate what you read and apply it in your daily life – even in a small way.

With perseverance, consistent reading and application, you will begin to experience the magic of faith in your life!

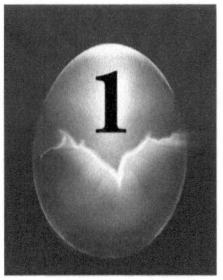

THE CONTEXT OF FAITH AND BELIEFS

This part of the book introduces the context and relevance of faith. It explains the role that beliefs play in our lives and how faith relates to beliefs.

1
FAITH AND BELIEF

There was once a young man, who liked to travel to places. His life was all about traveling. No sooner did he hear about an interesting place than he would set off to see it. High mountains, deep valleys, dense jungles, raging rivers, he had seen it all.

Just when he started to feel that he had seen just about everything, during one of his travels, he landed up in a desert. Such an arid and desolate desert as he had never seen before. Sand dunes extending in every direction as far as he could see. He walked and walked to no end.

Soon his supplies were exhausted and he got desperate to drink water. He had heard of the horrors of deaths in the desert due to dehydration, but he could see no sign of water or even the slightest moisture anywhere. No houses, no camps, no animals, not a single human being, just sand everywhere.

Just then, he saw something that looked like a hand pump. Not believing his eyes, he mustered all the remaining energy in his body and ran towards to it. He couldn't believe his eyes. It really was a hand pump! Thanking his stars, he grabbed the scorching handle of the pump and began working. Alas! Nothing came out of the outlet! He worked the pump even more frantically but it only made noise… and nothing!

He fell down on his knees knowing this to be his end when his eyes caught a little bottle that was tied to a wooden stump near the pump. What was it that his eyes saw in that bottle? Could it be water? It was! It was water. He grabbed the bottle and was about to gulp the water down when he saw a note on the wooden stump. It read:

"NOTE: Do not drink this water. Pour it into the pump so that the pump works and then you can have as much water as you want!"

It was such a risk! He was holding a bottle full of water that he had found after being so close to death and if he wanted more, he had to risk it. Would the pump work after he risked pouring the water in it? Wouldn't it be better to just drink the water he had right now? But if he drank the water in the bottle, there would be none left for the next traveler - neither to drink, neither to pour into the pump!

Should he have just drank the water in the bottle and quenched his thirst? Or should he have poured it into the pump and risked the one chance of survival he had?

Now, this is the question that we should ask ourselves: "What would I do? Would I trust what was written on the note at the risk of dying of dehydration? Or would I trust life? Would I have the courage and assurance to consider why someone would leave a bottle of water in the middle of the scorching desert with this note?"

Finally, the young man made up his mind. He decided to keep faith in whoever had written the message. He walked the long five meters towards the pump with the bottle in his trembling hands and poured it all into the pump. He then grabbed the handle and worked it even more desperately than before. Nothing for the next few long seconds that seemed like ages. A feeling of fear gripped him. Had he blundered? He decided to wait and watch.

And then it happened! With a splashing sound the water gushed out. What a miracle! So much water... as much as he could drink, bathe and carry! He rushed to hold his hands under the flowing water to assure himself that he was not hallucinating! Cold water in such a hot desert – it was a strange contrast!

He drank till he could drink no more, drenched himself in the water and filled up his water bags. A little while later, when he was feeling much more like his lively self, he got up to leave. Before he left, he grabbed the board with the note on the stump and wrote under it, "It works!", smiled and walked away!

Faith is at the core of our existence. It is the nature of our very essence that lies latent, waiting to be expressed to its highest potential. Faith is the most potent power given to man. It is only when we express faith that we truly get a sense of accomplishment and contentment in our lives.

It is the highest vibration in the universe. It is what all religions are based on. And yet, **faith is not the product of any particular religious belief. Faith is not *owned by* any particular religion. Faith transcends all religious dogma.** Though the word 'faith' has been used synonymously with 'religious belief or following', it goes beyond all beliefs. It is the very fiber of our being. It is the driving essence of life; life cannot exist without faith.

Beliefs and Illusory Reality

Before we get into understanding faith and its guiding principles, let us first understand more about beliefs and how they differ from faith. It is common for many people to consider the two to mean the same. Though they are interrelated, making them very close in meaning, yet there's a big difference.

Our beliefs are ideas that we are thoroughly convinced of. As they are ideas or concepts that we gather through information and experience, our beliefs can change over time as we gain more knowledge and new experiences during our lives.

The beliefs that we hold within us create an illusory reality, which we assume as our personal truth. This illusory reality hides the 'real' reality from us. Illusory reality is like a mental lens that is shaded by our beliefs. It distorts our experience of life.

You can imagine this lens as a skewed magnifying lens, which tends to magnify certain things and minimize the importance of certain other things. It may magnify something trivial, while minimizing something important. As a result, our experience of life could perhaps appear worrying and sorrowful.

Our beliefs are the foundation of our lives. They are the framework that determine how we experience and express in our life. When we are born, we may have an initial set of beliefs that we inherit from parents. As we grow up, we build further on our beliefs by borrowing them from our parents, our neighbors, friends, from school, from our surroundings, and most importantly from the Media.

Social media has become the primary factor in determining how we perceive the world. Today, many of us tend to inadvertently borrow our opinions from online communities. When these opinions are held within us for some time, they get ingrained as beliefs.

Beliefs also create a self-image within the subconscious mind, which we assume as 'I'. It is as if whatever happens to this fictitious image, happens to 'me'. There are innumerable limiting beliefs that define the 'I' that we assume for ourselves. "I don't deserve," "I am not enough," "I am not lovable," "Things come hard in my life," "I cannot trust people," etc.

If we carefully observe, it is not difficult to see that such beliefs are not always true, but we hold onto them and shade our experience of life through them. We find it difficult to let go of them because they define us, or rather, they define and limit our self-image.

We are not our self-image. The self-image is a mask that we have donned. "I am weak," "I am a victim," "I am unhappy." All these qualifiers that follow "I am…" keep changing with time, but the "I am…" always remains the same. "I am" is the simple truth that we can consider as who-we-truly-are, beyond the changing persona. "I am" is pure being; that's what we essentially are.

Who you *think* you are is actually a self-image; who you *truly* are is pure being.

The persona or self-image is like a costume that "I am" wears. Just as clothing does not define a person, the persona is not who we truly are. In some way, the persona does help us in relating to people and situations. But, most of it is a bundle of accumulated beliefs and stories, that largely do not serve our wellbeing. The real "I" has been reduced to a limited personalized "I" that can struggle and feel victimized by life.

The lens of beliefs creates an illusory reality. If we could look within and introspect the beliefs that make us see reality in a distorted way, we could get rid of them. But, beliefs are reinforced by the emotions that they trigger and the evidences that they manifest.

Emotions like fear, anger, guilt or sorrow are sensed in various parts of the body as physical sensations. They can be sensed as discomfort in the belly, pressure in the chest, heat in the eyes and ears, or pain in the shoulders. The past conditioning of the subconscious mind triggers these sensations and evokes thoughts and impressions from similar past occurrences. They make the beliefs that trigger them feel real. The illusory reality is strengthened by thoughts that reflect our beliefs and the emotions triggered by these thoughts.

Beliefs are self-fulfilling prophecies. A self-fulfilling prophecy is a belief that is actually not true, but becomes true merely because it is believed. Beliefs shape our perception. They cause us to see reality in a particular way by distorting certain aspects of our experience. This distorted perception shapes our responses to people and situations; it determines our actions. In turn, our responses and actions result in rebounds that further reinforce our beliefs.

> For a long period of time, experts believed that the human body was incapable of achieving a four-minute mile i.e. running a distance of one mile in four minutes. It wasn't just difficult, it was outright impossible. People tried for many years to achieve a four-minute mile, but in vain. It came to be known as the "four-minute barrier."
>
> Then in the 1940's the record was pushed to 4:01. It was close, but still not technically a four-minute mile. This record stood

for nine years! Athletes all over the world began to believe that the experts were right – that the four-minute mile was in fact an impossible feat.

But Roger believed otherwise. He firmly believed that he could achieve not only a four-minute mile, but even a sub-four-minute mile. He believed this with such fiery passion that it was already a reality for him. He knew it to be true in his heart. Finally, on May 6th, 1954, Roger set a new record of 3:59.4. This was the famous athlete Roger Bannister. He achieved this feat not merely due to his training and physical prowess, but by the extraordinary strength of his belief.

Surprisingly, his record was broken only 46 days later by another runner who completed the mile in 3:58 minutes. Since then over 1,400 athletes have achieved a sub-four-minute mile over the years!

What was considered an impossible feat by people all over the world for over nine years, suddenly became possible because one person broke the mental limitation for so many others! By completing a mile within four minutes, Roger had given other compatriots an evidence of the belief that it *can* be done.

People *experienced* the fact that an athlete was actually able to run the mile under four minutes. This faith paved the way for many others to achieve not only the same, but even better feats. It is interesting to note that the lowest time recorded so far is 3:43.13!

Note how it was the belief of a single person that something impossible was do-able. In this person also, this belief started off as a mere thought, which was then nurtured into a belief through constant repetition and visualization. When others saw the evidence of the outcome of Roger's faith, they were able to believe in it themselves. One person's faith made something that was considered impossible, achievable for everyone!

Beliefs are like roofs. A roof cannot stand by itself; it needs pillars. The roof of belief needs pillars of evidence. If it doesn't have those pillars, it will collapse. The more evidence you acquire, the more pillars you provide for the roof of belief, the stronger it becomes. You get evidences for whatever you choose to believe.

Given enough time, a strange thing happens. The roof of belief becomes so strong that it doesn't require the pillars of evidence any longer. It stands on its own. In effect, the belief has become your indisputable truth.

For example, consider the belief that people are not trustworthy. This belief tends to cause a mindset of suspicion and insecurity. People around sense these feelings at the subconscious level and respond in the same measure. Their responses serve as evidences that in turn strengthen this belief. The belief that people are not trustworthy makes it likely that we zoom in on instances where people betray our or others' trust. It neglects instances where people live up to the trust that is placed on them.

Thus, the external world is merely a reflection of the beliefs that we hold within. If we can change our beliefs, we can change our experience of life. We can change how the world appears to us.

How Belief Grows into Faith

> Anita's father was a very important figure for her and his words meant a great deal to her. One day, when Anita was a young school student, she heard her father talk to someone, "This world is full of cheats. It is difficult to trust anybody!". His words sunk in and this little belief took root in her young and impressionable mind. This was just something she had heard her father say. It was not her own experience; however, soon it was going to be!
>
> As it so happened later in her life, there came situations where Anita was expecting help from her friends, but they couldn't help her. Now, although there were genuine reasons why her friends couldn't be of help in the given situation, her belief that, "One cannot trust anybody!" that had already made home in her mind, grew stronger. Gradually, as this belief grew stronger, she continued to get experiences that mirrored her belief. Taking them as evidences to corroborate her belief, she grew more and more skeptical about people.

What do we understand from this? A belief is born from a simple thought that is a result of something we hear or read somewhere. When we notice the evidences of the belief in our lives, it becomes our faith. The belief manifests itself in the form of an experience. In other words, it can be said that your faith in something develops when a belief is evidenced through first-hand experience.

Imagine you are walking down a road one cold winter morning. In the biting cold, you feel glad that you have a nice winter jacket that keeps you warm. And then you see how the homeless and penniless are barely surviving in such conditions. Just as you are thinking about this, you notice a man handing out blankets to beggars crouching on the pavement. You like what you see and it fills you with a warm feeling - warmer than the blanket! A thought passes by your mind that "There are people in this world, who are so helpful!".

When this thought arises within you from your direct perception of what you saw, there are good chances that you will continue to see more people helping others. It is highly probable that you might even receive help when in need, all because of this belief of yours.

It is an irrefutable law of nature that whatever you believe and feel to be true long enough, will become your reality. It means that whatever you are convinced and assured of at the deepest level of your inner world of beliefs will always show up in your outer world. If you believe people are good, nature makes sure you meet good people.

This implies that **whatever happens to a person is a direct result of their own beliefs, not of external circumstances**. It does not matter what others believe. If you believe it with conviction, it will show up.

2
EVERYTHING IS A GAME OF BELIEFS

A sales executive always believed that he suffered from motion sickness. As soon as he would feel the motion of the vehicle, he would feel dizzy, nauseated and the churning in his stomach. When he took a pill, he would immediately feel relieved. On one such occasion, he was given a plain sugar pill instead of his usual pill, but he still felt better. What made him feel better on this occasion?

When American surgeon Henry Beecher was treating wounded American soldiers during World War II, he ran out of pain-killing morphine. Out of sheer desperation to save them, he injected them with a saline solution instead of morphine. To his surprise, the solution worked as a pain-killer for around 40% of soldiers and he could operate on them successfully. How could these soldiers endure the intolerable pain with a saline solution?

An experiment was conducted on two people who suffered from headaches. The first subject was given a pain-killing medicine and the second was given a sugar pill. They were also told the same. However, while administering those pills, they were interchanged without their notice. The sugar pill was enclosed in the garb of a pain-killer and the pain-killer was given as a sugar pill. Now, the one who took the sugar pill in the garb of the pain killer soon felt relieved of the headache, while the other continued to suffer the headache, believing that the sugar pill couldn't cure him. What caused these diametrically opposite results?

A healthy man went for a health check-up. Due to human error, his reports got exchanged with that of a cancer patient. To his utter shock, he read that his cancer was at an advanced stage and that he had only six months left. Soon he developed symptoms of dizziness, weakness and weight loss. He started counting days. He was admitted to a hospital due to multiple health complications. When his tests were re-done, of course, human error won't always repeat! Everyone was astonished to find that he never had cancer to begin with. The supposed disease that had tormented him, was not there at all! Why then did he suffer?

What do these examples from real life indicate?

If we believe in something or anticipate some outcome, our expectation induces an active stimulus in our brain, which then affects the cells of our body including the brain. Sometimes, our genes can also get affected due to our beliefs. A change in our beliefs can bring about a transformative change in our behavior, our experience of life, and even our physiology.

Our beliefs also result in the formation of neural pathways in our brain. Every belief has a behavior and a feeling associated with it. The association of every belief, feeling and behavior is stored in memory. Whenever we repeat the belief, the associated feeling and behavior also get triggered, making us experience it in the same way every time. The more we have faith in our beliefs, the more evidences we get, and the more our beliefs get reinforced.

The good news is that by merely changing our beliefs, we can witness changes in our feelings and behavioral patterns. As we saw in the second example, the soldiers believed that they were injected with a pain-killer instead of a mere saline solution; hence they could endure the intolerable pain. This shows how desired changes can be brought about in the body cells when a new belief is induced in our minds.

Depending upon the belief induced in the brain, anticipated results are experienced in the body. If the belief is positive, the results are positive and vice versa. The Placebo effect and the Nocebo effect are based on this principle. The Placebo effect has been widely used in psychology and medicine.

The phenomenon, in which the recipient perceives an improvement in condition due to positive expectations, rather than the treatment itself, is known as the placebo effect or the placebo response.

On the contrary, the phenomenon in which the recipient's condition worsens due to his negative expectations, rather than treatment or causative element is called the nocebo effect.

A placebo can be a substance, or treatment, or even a suggestion with no active therapeutic effect. Common placebos include sugar pills, saline water, etc. They are commonly used in cases involving pain, depression, anxiety, fatigue, etc. As we saw in the above examples, people were cured when they were administered a placebo medicine.

- In example 1, the pill acted as a placebo. The person's strong belief about having motion sickness made him feel dizzy and nauseated. But as soon as he gulped the pill, he felt better. The pill worked in his favor because he strongly believed that the pill would cure him.

- In example 2, the saline solution acted as a placebo. The soldiers could endure pain because they strongly believed the saline solution to be a pain killer. Thus, even though they were not injected with a pain killer, their positive belief helped them to endure the severe pain successfully.

- In example 3, the person gulped a sugar pill in the garb of a pain-killer. He believed that the pain killer would give him relief and the belief worked. He was cured of his headache. The sugar pill acted as a placebo for him.

The Nocebo effect is when a negative outcome is observed in life as a result of negative beliefs and expectations. The nocebo effect is illustrated in examples 3 and 4.

- In example 3, the other person believed the pain-killer to be a sugar pill. He believed that a sugar pill cannot cure him and his belief nullified the effect of the pain-killer. As a result, he didn't experience relief from his headache.

- In example 4, the healthy person believed that he had cancer. Hence, his body immediately threw up the symptoms of cancer, even though there was no cancer.

If you want to change your life, you need to change your beliefs. You need to inculcate new positive healthy beliefs, which will in turn act as a placebo. The more you repeat these belief statements passionately and frequently with faith and feeling, the more strength they gain to manifest into reality.

Harmony in your feelings, thoughts, speech and actions boosts these beliefs to manifest in your life. Very soon, repetition of these positive healthy beliefs will change the blueprint of your mind. The cells of your body including the brain can change too. Your genes too can change! When this understanding is applied, attaining physical fitness, mental peace, social harmony, financial abundance and spiritual wellbeing will become possible.

Suppose that you tell yourself, "Whenever I eat yogurt, I become healthier." Research proves that even if you know that this is a placebo, it will still produce the desired result.

> Recent scientific research explains how the human DNA can be influenced and re-programmed by words without the need for intervention in the physical plane. Only 10% of our DNA is used for building proteins. Till recently, the other 90% was considered "junk DNA." However, recent collaborative research by linguists and geneticists discovered that the apparently useless 90% of the human DNA is not only responsible for constructing our bodies but also serves as means for data storage and communication. It contains encoded data that follows the same grammar rules of syntax and semantics as our human languages. So, the evolution of human languages is not a coincidence, but rather a reflection of our inherent DNA. Due to this, human DNA resonates with human language.

It turns out that we can use words and sentences to influence living DNA! This has been experimentally proven. DNA present in living tissue responds to language-modulated inputs. This scientifically explains why affirmations and auto-suggestions have such strong effects on our bodies and physiology. Spiritually evolved souls have known since ages that our body is programmable by words and thought. This is now beginning to gain scientific ground.

In order to repeat these positive belief statements, you may write them down in your diary and read them aloud. You may repeat them in a relaxed posture, either sitting on a chair or lying down on the bed. The potency of spoken words increases manifold when your body is relaxed. When you repeat these statements with faith and love, they get instilled in your mind immediately. You may also sing them to yourself in a melodious tune. Melody is an infallible catalyst for creating deep positive impressions in the mind.

You also need to become aware of the nocebo effect in your life. Are negative expectations creating negative outcomes in your life? For instance, are you telling yourself, "I am getting old, so I am losing enthusiasm"? If this is the case, you are falling prey to the nocebo effect. You need to affirm to yourself that your physical age has nothing to do with your mental age.

Role of Placebo and Nocebo effects in Life

Since our childhood, we have nurtured fixed beliefs by observing our parents, friends, neighborhood and the media. Most of us believe them without questioning their authenticity. By reading or watching news, we tend to believe we can be victims to the happenings of the world.

Many of us lead a constricted life that is fraught with fear, uncertainty and insecurity. Many believe that this is how life will be forever. Their belief manifests in their lives. Our beliefs have created the world we live in now. If we are experiencing discontent, sorrow and failure, it is because these beliefs have acted as a nocebo in our lives. Most people believe that their life situations and people are the culprit for their miseries and try hard to correct them, but to no avail.

When we question these deep-seated beliefs, we may find that they are no longer valid. The truth may be completely different. We need to re-think our beliefs and command the body that it can completely heal itself by releasing these beliefs that do not serve us. It is possible to be free from all such core beliefs.

It is not a sugar pill that cures, but the change in our thoughts. Knowing this, we can have faith that just by changing our thoughts, we can also heal ourselves. If we are experiencing the same situations again and again, then it is only because the same thoughts have been unconsciously repeated within us.

Once we identify the limiting beliefs within, we can replace them with new positive thoughts, which align with love, joy, peace and harmony. Whenever negative beliefs come into play, we need to instruct ourselves that we don't need them now and can delete them. If we have been in their favor, we can firmly resolve to be in favor of positive beliefs, which will have a positive healing effect in life.

With this, you can soon see that a new reality will manifest. For example, if you were harboring hatred for someone due to your old belief, you will feel compassion for the same person due to your changed positive belief. Thus, despite the situation being the same, just by changing your beliefs, your experience of life can change too.

Beyond Placebo and Nocebo

As we experiment with positive beliefs and begin to see a positive transformation, we can consider breaking free from the cocoon of all our limiting beliefs. But for that, we need to learn to see the truth as it is without being swayed by a placebo or a nocebo. We can then be free from the influence of all the placebos and nocebos in life.

The greatest nocebo is that we have forgotten who-we-truly-are. We have believed ourselves to be limited individuals, thereby leading a constricted life. But as we begin to experientially know our true nature, the true Self or Pure consciousness, we become free from this illusion. This happens with the blossoming of the ultimate faith.

When you get established in the firm conviction that all the beliefs – whether positive or negative – are with your body and mind, not with you; that who-you-truly-are stands apart from them, then you can watch their effect on your body-mind with equanimity and alertness.

With every response that arises from a belief, you will witness it arising, staying for some time, and then dissolving. You will recognize the temporary nature of the play of these beliefs. As you consistently watch this rise and fall, they will gradually dissolve.

As you lead a life free of beliefs and tendencies, you will experience joy in the midst of all circumstances. Thereafter, the infinite potential of the true Self begins to express through your body-mind. You start leading a fresh life of abundance, health, wealth, harmony, joy, creativity and positivity.

A life, free from beliefs, is a stress-free life, where everything happens spontaneously in perfection. Even if few people bring it out into practice, they can bring about a positive change in the world.

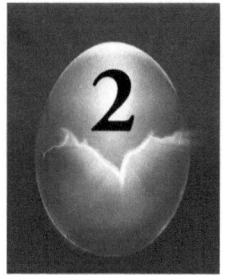

PRINCIPLES OF FAITH

The Power of Faith rules all of creation. It determines how life unfolds. In this part of the book, we will consider the principles by which we can guide our lives, so as to align ourselves with this highest vibration in the universe.

3

PRINCIPLE 1

THE FAITH FRAME

Faith is the feeling of deep assurance in life. At an obvious level, it is the conviction that we invest in our beliefs, but it is much more profound than that. Faith is the force that brings our beliefs into fruition. When we completely trust something without doubt, we are exercising our faith. And it doesn't take much of faith to witness huge, even miraculous happenings.

In the words of Jesus, "If one tells the mountain to be taken up and thrown into the sea, and has no doubt at all in his heart, but believes that what he says will come to pass, it will be done for him. Whatever you ask in prayer, believe that you have received it, and it will be yours."

When we contemplate and understand the true potential of faith, we realize that faith makes anything possible. With this realization, we are able to overcome all doubts, suspicions and hesitation that grip our minds. However, until that stage is reached, our faith is unstable.

We were all born with the power of faith already ingrained within us. It cannot be said that any particular person has no faith at all. Of course, what varies is *what* a person has faith in.

Consider a person who has a thousand dollars to invest. There are two investment options. He could divide the sum equally between the two options or have an uneven distribution. He could even have the whole sum invested in one of the options. That's up to him.

In some way, faith is like this money that we have at our disposal. Note that the quantum of faith remains the same all our life; but whether we invest it in positivity or in negativity - that can vary.

To understand how faith works, let us understand the Faith Frame. Imagine a square frame. The four corners of the square represent Faith, Feelings, Actions and Results. These are the four aspects of how life manifests.

The four sides of this Faith frame represent how the four aspects relate to each other:

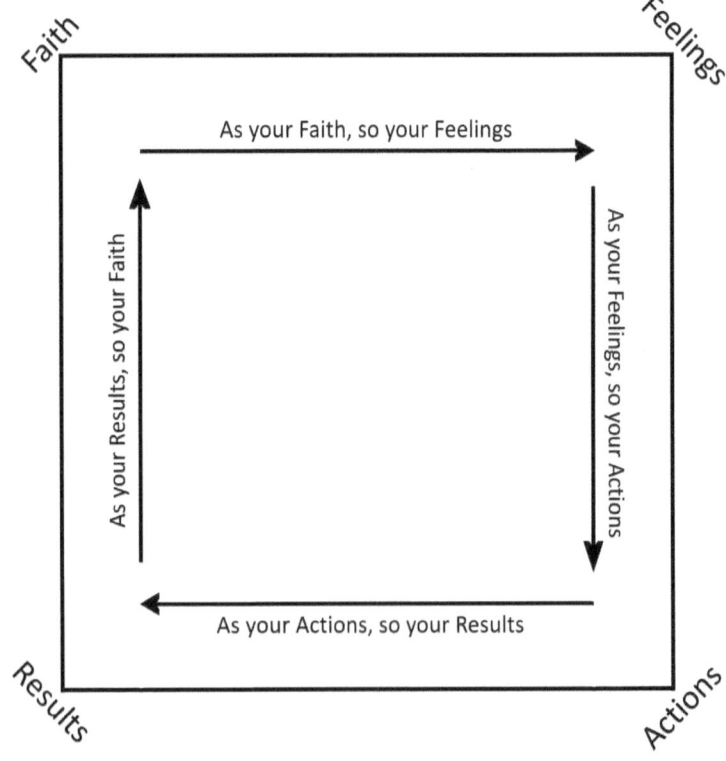

1. **As your Faith, so your Feelings**
2. **As your Feelings, so your Actions**
3. **As your Actions, so the Results**
4. **As the Results, so your Faith**

This is the first principle of faith.

Our lives are driven by this Faith Frame, which keeps varying in size. Sometimes it grows large and sometimes it diminishes. At any given time in life, everything that happens with us, is a direct function of the state of our Faith Frame at that given time.

The Faith Frame indicates how our faith determines how we feel about anything, which in turn bears on our actions, consequently begetting their result or outcome. The intriguing thing here is that the results that we get in life also influence our faith – they may either reinforce our faith in something, or reduce it. This can also be called the Faith cycle.

Let's go a step further and understand that there are two kinds of faith cycles: a negative faith cycle and a positive faith cycle. A negative faith cycle begins with faith invested in a negative belief, while a positive one begins with our faith invested in a positive belief.

Let us consider a simplified example of a sports match between Team A and Team B to understand these two faith cycles.

Negative Faith Cycle

Let us say that the match is taking place in City A which is the hometown of Team A. The match is at a point where Team A is rapidly gaining on Team B. Because the match is taking place in City A, maximum fans are rooting for Team A. The cheers and slogans being shouted in support of Team A are far louder.

In such a scenario, the players of Team B begin to lose confidence. Both the teams had begun the match with the same faith that they can win. However, as the situation progresses, Team B's faith shifts from "We are going to win the match" to "We are going to lose!" Notice the beginning of a negative faith cycle with faith that shifts to a negative belief.

With this negative faith taking root in their minds, their emotional state responds with feelings of despair and lowered morale. These feelings reflect in the way the players are playing their game. They make mistakes, take shots that they shouldn't, miss simple opportunities. Notice how their feelings are influencing their actions. As an outcome of their actions, Team B's position in the match worsens. Their score drops further down and this reinforces their negative faith that "We are going to lose!"

We can see how the cycle starts with a negative belief and how everything that follows leads to the reinforcement of their faith in that belief. The same cycle goes on till the negative belief manifests fully and Team B actually loses the match.

Positive Faith Cycle

Consider the state of Team A through the same situation. As they slowly gain a winning position, their faith - that they can win the match - strengthens. This positive faith makes them feel energetic, excited and happy. These feelings lead them to perform efficiently and effectively on the field. They are able to put in all their energy into the game, making all the right moves. These actions give them the expected results and their position in the game keeps improving. And as their position improves, their faith, that they can win, gets stronger.

Notice in the case of Team A, how a little positive faith strengthens as the positive faith cycle repeats itself. Both the teams began with the same faith - that they can win. Later on, in the game too, Team B lost, not because they did *not* have faith. They lost because their faith shifted from a positive belief to a negative one. Towards the end of the match, both the teams had faith, however the difference was the belief in which they had placed their faith.

Steadfastness of Faith

In the above example, imagine a scenario in which Team B's faith *hasn't* shifted to a negative belief; both the teams have continued to have faith in the same positive belief - that they can win. Having the same faith, both the teams would be going through a positive faith cycle. Who then would eventually win the game?

In such cases, what becomes the winning factor or the key to success is the steadfastness of faith. We saw at the beginning of the chapter, how the Faith Frame keeps changing in size. It grows in one situation, but diminishes in the other. These are signs of a faltering faith; one that is affected by external incidents and outcomes.

A good result or a desired outcome leads to a growing Faith Frame. Anything undesirable happens and the Faith Frame diminishes. In other words, faith is not steadfast; it falters. It is subject to externalities; the outcomes of actions - either our own or those of others. This dependency on the outcome is what causes the faith to falter. One is not able to have faith in the positive without tangible proofs. In other words, it is difficult for most of us to believe in the *unseen*. Faith in the unseen comes with a clear understanding of who-we-truly-are and conviction of the way life works. We shall discuss more about faith in the unseen, later in this book.

Transitioning the Faith Cycle

So far, we have seen how believing in a little idea - positive or negative - starts the faith cycle. Upon analyzing one's life, one might feel that they are stuck in a negative cycle, which began with a little negative belief, which has now grown into a sticky life pattern.

> Sarah had been giving interviews for a job since nearly six months, but she was not able to land a job. With every rejection, the negative faith kept getting stronger. Her faith, feelings, actions and outcomes were all getting increasingly negative. It was high time that Sarah made a transition from a negative faith cycle to a positive one. But how could she achieve this?

To shift from a negative faith cycle to a positive cycle, one can choose any one of the four corners of the Faith Frame, viz. Faith, Feelings, Actions, or Results.

After having chosen the corner that suits best, one has to consciously work on it and give it a positive push. Gradually, with this small shift, the faith cycle can reverse to being positive.

Let us understand how we can work with either of the four corners of the Faith Frame.

Working on Faith: If one chooses the corner of Faith to shift the cycle, one can concentrate on consciously shifting one's faith from the negative idea to a positive idea. In the case of Sarah, she can consciously shift her faith from "I can't get a decent job" or "I am a failure at giving interviews" to "I can and will get the perfect job that's designed for me at the right time" or "I am getting better and better at handling interviews."

Before this shift, she was convinced that she is a failure. It is a law of nature that whatever you focus on begins to grow until it consumes you completely. The negative idea - though very little at first - had grown to be the reality of her life. However, she could shift to focus on the positive idea instead, allowing it to slowly grow as per the law of nature. For this, she had to plant the new belief, deep in her subconscious mind.

The next chapter discusses the Seed of Faith and how it can be planted at the depth of the subconscious mind.

Working on Feelings: To work on this corner, one has to make oneself aware of the feelings that are aroused by a negative belief. Anger, depression, sadness, remorse, guilt – whatever the emotion may be – one has to consciously observe it. Next, one should repeat a positive idea in their mind and feel the emotion that the positivity arouses. In other words, learn to turn the negative emotions into an opportunity, a ladder.

If Sarah chooses to work on her emotions, she should observe the emotions that are aroused by her failure at interviews. Fear, despair, dejection – she should bring all these feelings to the centerstage of her consciousness. She will begin to notice how these emotions are affecting her on the physical and mental planes. She should then repeat affirmations like, "I have already secured my dream job and am thoroughly satisfied with the way it has turned out", which trigger positive feelings within.

Working on Actions: Those who choose to work on their actions should begin doing things that will help them achieve their positive goal. A student who is trying to get better at his studies needs to stop watching TV or browsing the internet aimlessly. He can give up the redundant use of gadgets. He can form study groups and prepare systematic schedules to cover topics of study. A professional trying to get better at work can begin by categorizing his tasks and taking them to completion. He can set aside a certain time period every day to conduct research regarding his field of work to gain expertise. One has to begin taking concrete steps, which in turn begins the reversal of the negative faith cycle.

If Sarah chooses to work on her actions, she should begin preparing for interviews by conducting online research, by meeting people who are good at giving interviews. She can ask her close friends or relatives to help her by taking a mock interview. She can prepare for interviews by researching the company that she is appearing for the interview at; finding out what the company is into and using that knowledge in the interview. These are actions that will begin taking her closer to her goal.

Working on Results: This is perhaps the most sublime corner of the Faith Frame that one can choose to work on. If one spends enough time perfecting this corner, the Faith Frame can be transformed from being a square into a triangle – the state of transcendence of the Faith Frame! This is discussed at length later in this book. For now, let us understand how one can work on the *Outcomes* corner of the Faith Frame to turn the cycle around.

It is a human tendency to feel happy when their actions bear desirable outcomes and feel sad and disheartened when they don't. It is common for many of us to question God's intentions and call him names when we receive setbacks in our lives.

However, when one chooses to work on this corner of the Faith Frame, one has to teach oneself to view every outcome – whether desirable or otherwise – as a step closer towards one's goal. This also means that one has to have faith in what is unseen. The undesirable outcome is only a visible link in a series of happenings that will culminate in the realization of the final goal.

Every time Sarah gets rejected in an interview, she should receive that outcome gracefully. She needs to take it – though blaringly negative – as a step towards her goal. Her mantra should be, "Every rejection prepares me better for the next opportunity."

It is up to each one to choose the corner they want to work on. Some find it easier to work with faith, while some might consider it easier to work on their actions. Some might even find it feasible to work on their perception of outcomes.

Whichever corner we choose, the result remains the same: the reversal of the faith cycle. By bringing about even a small shift in either of these, we can bring about a great change in our lives.

4
PRINCIPLE 2
THE SEED OF FAITH

Whatever we hear, see and experience from our childhood, becomes a seed that gets sown within us. We begin to believe in our feelings and thoughts to such an extent that they become our personal reality. Every thought that we agree with, every idea that we find convenient – whether positive or negative, whether purposefully or inadvertently – becomes a *seed of faith*, a seed that grows to define our life.

Children who grow up watching their parents help others unconditionally, grow up to have a helping nature themselves. Whenever they are in a situation where someone around them needs help, they spontaneously respond, because they grew up with that seed within them. They've heard their parents say, "We should be kind and helpful to people." They have seen their parents demonstrating it. Hence, they never doubt that instinct when they grow up.

To cite another example, children who grow up watching their parents struggle financially, inadvertently grow up to have negative thoughts and feelings themselves. The thoughts of lack, "We don't have enough", "Life is not easy" and "It's not easy to lead a comfortable life" become seeds of faith for them. Unless they are able to change their thoughts and feelings and in turn their beliefs, it is highly likely that they remain poor and struggle all their life. To break free of their reality, they will need to sow new seeds of faith by giving their thoughts and feelings a positive twist.

On the other hand, children who belong to families where their parents have exuded abundance, grow up with the seed of faith that they have abundant money and other essential resources. For this reason, the chances of their keeping rich or getting richer is high.

This forms the basis for the famous quote, "The Haves shall continue to have and the Have-nots shall continue to not."

Each person goes through various phases of life and encounters different people and situations. It is up to each one to decide what to let inside their heart. Whichever thought or belief the person lets inside becomes a seed of faith for them and it manifests in their future.

If a person experiences a sad event like the passing away of a close and dear relative, what belief would he nurture within? If he nurtures the belief that the world is full of sorrow and there is suffering everywhere, that becomes his seed of faith and his future manifests in a way that reinforces that belief. One may not nurture a negative belief on purpose; it may be inadvertent, but it will bear fruits all the same.

Think of the seeds of faith that are advertently or inadvertently planted when people excessively indulge in watching news channels and crime stories. It is a common tendency that people are quick to believe a bad or negative news, whereas a positive one is looked upon with suspicion.

For example, if there was a news about a player who accepted a bribe to lose a game, most people would be very quick to believe it, saying, "Yes, he did lose the game on purpose!" However, if there is news about a famous person helping the poor and needy, most people will express suspicion about the person's intent in helping others. They may probably even go to the extent of blaming the news channel for spreading false propaganda. The root of this tendency lies in the fact that most people have planted negative seeds of faith, due to which they tend to focus on negativity more easily than positivity.

Rabindranath Tagore, the celebrated Indian poet-laureate, has beautifully described Faith as "the bird that feels the light when the dawn is still dark."

Faith is present within every living being – be it animals, plants or humans. It is faith that makes birds chirp even before the break of dawn. It is faith that makes a seed germinate and sprout from the cracks of arid soil. Faith manifests itself through every living facet of nature.

You will find that all the other living beings, except humans, act in natural accordance with their inherent faith. It is only us humans that can act in contradiction to it. This is mainly because human faith is greatly influenced by what is perceived in the world – by the people we interact with, by the kind of environment we live in. This *influenced* faith, which is based on the illusory reality, defines our prospects, which then becomes our personal reality. In other words, we are able to believe only what we see. We find it difficult to trust the unseen.

The second principle of faith states: **First sow the seed of faith, then comes its fruit. Better the seed of faith, better its fruit.**

First the Seed, then the Fruit

Nature works on the principle of reciprocation. When you give something, you receive something. What you receive depends solely on what you give. You give positivity; you receive the same in return, and in great multiples.

Consider a young man, who works hard at studies, exercises regularly and nourishes his body with clean and simple food. For all his efforts, nature reciprocates by giving him good health and a stable income when he grows up. He gets what he gives. He has sown the right seeds and he reaps the benefits. The harder he works with good faith, the more effort he puts in, the better results he enjoys. If the young man were to say, let me get a nice job and good health first, only then I shall work hard at studies and eat good food, he's yet unaware of nature's modus operandi.

Consider the activities of a farmer. He tills the land, he sows quality seeds, waters and tends the soil and then allows nature to do its part. To get a quality yield, he puts in quality efforts. A farmer never says, "Let me see a good yield, let me be assured of it, only then shall I sow the seeds."

A person, who wants to donate to an orphanage, buys sub-standard supplies and groceries for them thinking, "It's an orphanage! Why do they need high quality groceries!" He even donates only such clothes that are torn and of no use to himself. Such a person should know that one can only expect results as good as the seeds one sows! If you want to do something, do it with all your heart and sincerity and it shall never go unrewarded.

People try to make a deal with God when they pray! "O Lord, please let me get promoted this year and I shall donate generously to charity." "O God, please bless me with a baby and I shall offer obeisance at the temple." "O Almighty, please land me that job and I shall serve food to a hundred people." Unfortunately, such people fail to understand that they cannot expect a yield before they sow the seeds. It is only when they sow the seed of faith that they will get a manifold return.

Sowing the seed of faith would mean taking appropriate actions towards the wish or goal we want to achieve and then leaving the rest to nature. Just like a farmer who sows the seed, tends the soil and then patiently waits for the harvest. He even expresses his faith by preparing for the harvest. Likewise, we should do everything in our power to strengthen our faith and then wait patiently while nature does its part.

There is also a subtle but important quality expressed by a farmer in the above example, that is worth mentioning in this context. After sowing the seeds, the farmer patiently waits to let nature do its part.

He doesn't get impatient to see the yield. He doesn't abandon the field midway because he doesn't see a yield when he expects to. He does not dig up the soil to check whether the seeds are germinating! His faith is steadfast. He keeps watering the sapling until the seeds sprout. Patience is the key quality that makes faith steadfast.

Better the Seed, Better the Fruit

There are people, who may have experienced that they did not get the expected results even after sowing the right seeds of faith.

The reason for that is that their faith lacks the quality of steadfastness. Faith has to be absolute, unquestionable, unconditional and unshakeable. If one wants to grow in his career, he cannot give up his quest due to a bad job interview. His faith, that he shall have a thriving career has to be steadfast, despite being weathered by failures.

It is important to gauge the quality of the seed. Better the seed, better is the fruit! But how do we gauge the quality of the seed of faith? What can be done to improve it?

All day long, we entertain numerous thoughts – some positive, some negative. We now know that every thought is potentially a seed of faith, but does *every single* thought manifest in our reality?

No! The only thoughts that will transform themselves into physical reality are those that are consciously directed. For this, the thoughts should have both awareness and passion associated with them.

Awareness and *passion* are the key; they are also the factors that influence the quality of the seed of faith. The seed of faith has to be tended with our awareness and happy feelings.

We must be conscious of the thoughts that arise. We must hold them in our awareness for them to manifest in our physical reality. Whatever we lend our awareness to, whatever we focus on, grows. For example, if one wants to be successful in a certain business, he should not treat the thought of success at business as just another stray thought. This thought has to be given special treatment. He has to hold it in his mind in the light of his awareness. He has to give all his focus to the thought, to empower it.

The second aspect is that of feelings. Only those thoughts that are powered by our passion and intention actually manifest. Hence to enhance the seed of faith, associate positive feelings with it. With strong intent, we must passionately believe in what we desire. Repeated contemplation generates the necessary feeling of passion. What we passionately feel makes a difference.

Conversely, when we hold negative feelings about what we want to attract in our lives, we are pushing what we want further away from us and keep it from happening. If, for example, someone constantly worries about money while intending to become wealthy, the negative feeling will supersede the positive thought. Hence it is important to always harbor positive feelings to ensure manifestation.

For example, suppose you are looking to improve your relationship with your spouse. Whenever you get some time in solitude, close your eyes and repeatedly tell yourself, *"Thank you for Love and Peace."* Imagine in your mind that the relationship between you and your spouse has already improved; experience the feeling that comes with it.

After opening your eyes, when you interact with your spouse, do not again get worked up if s/he does not respond the way you would like. Even if s/he were to say something that you perceive not to be loving, continue to harbor love and peace in your heart. Do not change the direction of your thoughts or alter your feelings. You may mentally keep saying, "Thank you for Love and Peace." By doing this, you are not only sowing the seed of faith for harmony in your relationship, but also improving your present with good feelings.

We have seen how sowing the seed of faith precedes getting the results. Also, better the quality of the seed, better is the result. Are you trying to bring about a profound change in your life? Are you trying to achieve results that may seem impossible or magical today? Begin with sowing the seed of faith. Sow it, nurture it, strengthen it and soon you shall see it flowering in your life!

How the Unseen Manifests

A seed germinates into a plant; a plant grows into a tree; it bears many fruits and flowers and most importantly, it bears seeds. Every single tree gives birth to many other trees of the same kind. This shows how every seed holds the potential of a jungle!

If one were to break open a seed, what would one find? Nothing! And yet, isn't it a wonder that the seed holds the potential to create a jungle! So is it with the seed of faith. There is nothing tangible that can be evidenced in holding onto faith. Yet, when you do hold onto faith, the results can be wondrous. You will find that a single individual life falls too short for the limitless bounty of miracles that can be received with the seed of faith.

Each one of us has the potential to become a good doctor, an innovative engineer, a successful businessman, a scientist or just about anything else that the person may aspire to be. The actions that the person undertakes towards achieving his goals have to be empowered by the seeds of faith. When actions are powered by faith, the manifestation comes faster and larger.

But what does "empowering one's actions with the seed of faith" mean? How do we do it? You do it by preparing for what you aspire for, ahead of time.

> A small village was going through a period of severe drought. Most of the villagers were farmers and since it was too small a village, it lacked elaborate irrigation facilities. The farmers' livelihood depended on rain and there had been no rain for many months. The wells had started drying up. The villagers were at their wits end about what could be done to relieve the situation. Finally, after all human effort had gone in vain, they surrendered and started praying for rain.

At a decided time, all the villagers – every single one of them – gathered in a large field to pray together. Just when they were about to begin the prayer, the village headman noticed a little girl walking towards the field with a little umbrella. The other villagers followed his gaze and also noticed her and were surprised to see her carrying an umbrella.

The little girl's father came forward from the crowd, a little embarrassed. He held his daughter's hands and said, "Why are you carrying an umbrella, my dear?"

The girl smiled, "You told me that so many people are going to pray for rain. So, I got an umbrella along so that I don't get wet on our way back home! Now that you asked me, why aren't the others carrying their umbrellas?"

The faith that the little girl had in the prayer was pure and more importantly unquestionable. She had no doubt whatsoever about the manifestation of the prayers, so much so that she prepared herself ahead of time, for the outcome and walked there with an umbrella! For her, it was a wonder why all the others weren't prepared for the eventual rain!

Here's another example to illustrate this:

Sofia was her college's running champion. She had been winning the first position for many years now. Her victory had become a routine for the students and school staff and yet the crowd cheered for her harder every year.

One year, Emma joined the college as a student. Emma was also a running enthusiast and she enrolled herself for the running competition at the annual sports fest. She worked hard at her running all year and finally the day of the race dawned.

Sofia had the confidence of a seasoned winner on her face as she walked onto the race track. As Emma and her friends walked towards the stands to keep their stuff, her friends noticed that Emma was carrying an extra bag. One of her friends inquired, "What are you carrying this empty bag for?"

"For the trophy!" said Emma without a moment's hesitation. "I need something to carry the trophy that I'm going to win today."

Her friends sneered behind her back! "How stupid of her!" they thought.

The race began and Sofia soon took the lead position as everyone expected. However, as the laps went by, Emma kept steadily gaining on her fellow runners. By the end of the second-to-last lap, she was only two positions behind Sofia. Sofia would glance back every now and then and see this new girl closing in on her.

The final lap started and by then Emma was right behind Sofia. It was now just between the two of them as the rest of the runners were left far behind. Emma put on a spurt of energy, stretched her legs to their fullest. Sprinting swiftly, she was soon gaining on Sofia. The finishing line came closer and Emma edged her head forward to meet the ribbon. She felt the ribbon give way and it all went crazy!

Emma had won! As the trophy was handed to her, everyone was shocked to see this new girl beat Sofia. Emma's friends were especially shocked.

Emma had worked hard at her running all year, but her actions were empowered by her faith. By taking an empty bag along, she had expressed her faith in her wish to win. It was her faith that had won.

Bringing an umbrella to a prayer for rain, bringing an empty bag to carry the trophy are all little actions that reinforce your faith seed. One who wishes to buy a car can buy a keychain for it in advance. A housewife who wants to buy a new fridge can free up space in her kitchen where she will place the new fridge. A person looking to buy a new home can buy a photo frame that he will put up in the hall. Someone looking to lose weight can buy clothes of the smaller size.

All these little actions act as seeds of faith. They help bring the unseen into manifestation. These are ways in which we can express our faith in the unseen. To put it in another way, these are ways in which we can chirp even before it is dawn!

Let us discuss an important question that begs an answer at this point.

What if the seed of faith does not bring about the manifestation of what we want, when we want it?

What if Emma had lost the race in the above example? Does it mean her faith was in vain? Does it mean the seeds were wasted? No! Failure only means that Nature wants you to prepare harder and better. It is an irrefutable fact that when you sow the seed of faith for whatever you want in life, it starts moving towards you. With time, it is bound to come to you.

However, if it doesn't come to you at a time when you expect it to, do not take that as a failure of your faith. It only means that you need to strengthen your faith.

Anything that appears as failure is actually a stepping stone. This means there is no such thing as failure. As a famous saying goes, "A rejection is nothing but God's protection, and a nudge in a better direction." Treat failure as a milestone in the journey to your destination. Failure is only showing you where you have reached so far and what it will take to reach your chosen destination.

Infinite possibilities exist in the unseen

Everything that has been created, is being created, and will be created, already exists as possibilities in the unseen, where it remains un-manifested. It remains unseen. There are immense possibilities. What manifests in the perceivable world is only a miniscule part of the unseen potential.

Hence, whenever we experience negativity or limitations, or are subject to troubling and demanding situations, it helps us to remember that these are only few of the infinite possibilities that exist in the unseen. This raises our awareness to the truth that divine qualities are available and can manifest, regardless of whatever negativity we see, feel, or hear.

We go through various life situations every day. Someone may say something that irritates us. We may feel let down because someone did not cooperate with us. We may be physically ill. Or we may be suddenly faced with a financial crisis.

In all these situations, the question is: **Do we react, or do we create?**

It is common for people to react to such situations by focusing on the negativity. However, they do not realize that they are placing their faith on what they don't desire and manifesting even more troubling situations by choosing to believe the illusion that they perceive.

Instead, we can convert the snake of negativity into a ladder for growth and new creation. We can choose to see higher possibilities, positive aspects in our mind's eye, when we are in the midst of such situations. This will plant seeds for the manifestation of a better future. All that we then need is to sow seeds of faith and patiently wait for miracles to occur.

In the next chapter, we will discuss how we can effectively plant the seed of faith in our lives. We will look at a powerful tool, a catalyst in manifesting our faith.

5
CATALYST TO MANIFEST THE SEED OF FAITH

For a seed to properly germinate and grow into a healthy plant, it is necessary for the seed to be planted at a certain depth under the soil. It wouldn't work to just scatter the seeds over the surface of the soil. Likewise, it is only when seeds of faith are planted at a certain depth within the mind that they bear fruit. Shallow faith is not effective in any way.

It is only when the seed of faith is planted in the depth of the subconscious mind that its potential can manifest.

But how do we achieve that? By persistent writing and conscious verbalizing. This practice serves as a catalyst to get an idea into the subconscious mind.

Written Words

All of us wish for a peaceful life. We all want to be successful in the physical, mental, financial, social and spiritual facets of our lives. One can be said to be holistically successful only if one has balanced success in each of these facets, not just a few. Having said that, how many of us can actually claim to have achieved success on every single facet? There are people who are physically fit but are financially unhealthy. Some have great prosperity but have poor relationships. Some have great relationships but are spiritually disoriented. Some have certain amount of success on all the facets but still feel a certain incompleteness within.

Most of us wish for complete success but end up achieving far less than what we had wished for. What is the reason for that? What is the most common reason for failure? Lack of clarity.

Most of us do not have clarity about exactly what we want and more subtly *why* we want it. This may sound illogical.

"How can I *not* know what I want from my life!" ... but it's true. At least that's what nature perceives from our thoughts, feelings, spoken words and actions.

A person wishes to own a luxury car. He even expresses his wish, but in comes the doubting mind.

"Can I really afford that car?"

"How am I going to pay for it?"

"My current income is less than half of what it should be to be even eligible for a loan!"

"Perhaps I should wish for a more affordable car?"

"But I like that one so much! No! I want that one!"

The expression of the wish is clouded by doubts and insecurity. In such a situation, we fail to express to nature *exactly what* we want so that it may manifest it for us. Wouldn't nature naturally feel, "This guy doesn't know what he wants!"? And the person ends up owning a car that is an average of all his mixed signals!

We make key decisions about how we intend to progress in various facets of life, about the kind of life we would love to lead and the things or qualities we wish to possess. But for many of us, all this remains a fantasy in our minds. We do not find enough time to write about *what* we aspire for, about *how* we have decided to live each day, and *why*.

The result of this is stress, disharmony, frustration, health problems, and a general lack of clarity that reflects in everyday situations. We don't achieve anything productive when we keep vacillating in our heads about what we really need and why. We are generally so caught up with everyday activities that most of us seldom find the time to think deeply about our goals, and even more so in writing.

If we truly understand the importance of having clarity about what we want, then we should be telling nature *exactly* what we want clearly and as descriptively as possible. That is where conscious and systematic writing comes in.

When we note down the details about what we plan to do, about what our deepest intentions are, and why we would like to live the way we wish to, we will begin to experience a newfound peace and clarity. Putting down our thoughts on paper helps us empty the unnecessary mental clutter and create space for new ideas and new possibilities to emerge.

The first step you can take to plant the seed of faith for whatever you wish in life at the subconscious level is to get into the habit of writing a Faith Diary. We can also call it a "Faith Fair Book".

What is a Faith Fair book and how is it different from the diaries that we usually write?

When people write diaries, they usually write about their past – the past day, the past year or some past experience. A diary is usually a record of things bygone. The Faith Fair book is just the opposite. A Faith Fair book is all about the future. You use it to clearly write everything that you wish in your future. In this chapter, we shall discuss certain thumb rules that you have to follow while you write your Faith Fair Book.

The Faith Fair Book is a tool that helps us gain clarity about what we really want in life and why. It is like a personal companion, that will accompany us every day, every moment, reminding us about our life choices, our key decisions, the principles that we live by.

Writing down your goal in precise detail increases the probability of getting there faster. It is an important law of nature that everything that manifests in reality first exists in the mental realm as a thought. Hence, when your thoughts are placed carefully on paper with full faith in nature's process, such writing serves as a seed of faith that catalyzes their manifestation.

What you write down after contemplation goes deep within your subconscious mind because you lend your attention to it. The subconscious mind gets programmed positively. Your thoughts, feelings, words and actions get aligned in the chosen direction. Your confidence and will power increases leading to positive results. This also helps in arousing positive feelings about the goal. Focused attention and enthusiasm are pivotal factors in realizing your goal.

Writing down your goals in precise detail is also the most effective way to gain clarity of what you truly want. Writing directs your attention to what you really want by de-focusing from what you don't want. Whatever you write in your Faith fair book serves an indication to nature that you genuinely want your goal to manifest in your life and then nature will also support you in this endeavor.

Clearly knowing what you want, why you want, and when you want, helps you evaluate when you are on track, or when you stray off track from the life path that you wish to take.

How to write the Faith Fair Book?

Each one of us has our own unique set of values and aspirations and the details of all of them have to go into the Faith Fair book. Let us look at some general pointers to be followed while you write your Faith Fair book.

Firstly, it's the *"Faith"* fair book because you write with full faith, thereby planting the seeds of faith for whatever you wish. When you write the Faith Fair book with unquestioning faith, you are bound to experience miraculous transformation in your life.

Secondly, it is the Faith *"fair"* book because it will be the distilled form of what you first write down roughly in scrap book. It helps to first write your needs in a rough scrapbook. This gives you flexibility to edit on-the-go.

It is required that you come up with your long-term goal after deep contemplation. Given this, ideally you wouldn't change your long-term goals, at least in the short or medium term. But if you still do, then you can surely update it in your Faith Fair book.

As you gain more understanding about how life works and clarity about what you really want, your writing gets continuously refined. You will keep revising your notes in the scrap book. The distilled version of what you write in the scrap book will be "faired" out into the "fair" book.

1. Maintain a single and detailed diary

The first rule is to use a single diary for your Faith Fair Book. Also, follow a systematic method of writing to avoid irritation later on. Without a systematic method, you might forget where you noted something important and might thereby waste time and effort in finding or re-writing it. Instead of a diary, you may also use your computer, tablet or mobile phone for efficiently managing your notes. Choose a medium that will help you keep numerous and detailed notes that can be readily searched and referred.

2. Divide your goals in categories

There are five planes of life: Physical, Mental, Financial, Social and Spiritual and we have to achieve success on all these planes. Every goal we have in life is related to one of these planes.

For example, wanting a better career or a bigger home or car is a goal related to the financial plane. Wanting better relationships is a Social goal. Wanting better health is a goal related to the physical plane. Someone who wants to work on his or her anger or depression is functioning on their mental plane. There will be people who want to know their true self and the ultimate purpose of their life. Such people need to work on their spiritual plane.

So, it helps to make five sections in the diary – one for each plane – categorize your goals and write every goal in the appropriate section.

Also, after having maintained the diary for a while, you will naturally come to the planes that you concentrate more on and the ones that are being neglected. You can then take up goals from the neglected planes so as to achieve a balanced and holistic success.

3. Write only What you Want; Not What you Don't

This is one of the most important pointers and probably the most common mistake that most people make when they pray or wish for something. Instead of expressing what they want, they inadvertently or otherwise, express what they *don't* want. Instead of praying "I want to be healthy," they pray, "I don't want to fall sick."

While writing the Faith Fair Book, you must focus only and only on what you want. Whatever you write in your Faith Fair book will become your reality. The subconscious mind does not understand "not" or "don't". It goes by the picture or feeling of what follows the "not" or "don't" and takes that as your chosen reality. Hence, use only wholesome, positive and inspirational words. Remember that positive words program your subconscious mind positively.

Here are a few examples:

Instead of: *I don't want to fall sick.*

Write: *I am enjoying the joy of good health.*

Instead of: *I don't want to be overweight (or obese).*

Write: *I want to be healthy, fit and lively with optimum body weight.*

Instead of: *I will need to work really very hard and take a lot of efforts to get the promotion.*

Write: *With proper disciplinary habits and adequate practice, I am easily earning the promotion.*

Instead of: *I don't want to be poor.*

Write: *I am blessed with abundance.*

In addition, you may write down the following affirmations for the different planes:

Physical Success

- I am enjoying good health and am feeling fit.
- I eat the right portion of right food at the right time.
- My healthy body is helping me attain the ultimate goal of my life.
- I feel slender and light.

Mental Success

- My mind is ever pure, peaceful, stable and filled with love for all of this creation.
- My mind is exuding positivity and zeal.
- My mind remains calm and composed, no matter what.

Social Success

- My relationships are brimming with harmony, love and trust.
- I am complete and content with my relationships.
- I am experiencing joy and lightness in all my interactions.

Financial Success

- I am making the right use of money to fulfil the true purpose of my life.

- Being successful is habitual and effortless for me.
- I am the source of prosperity and abundance.

Spiritual Success

- I am overflowing in the experience of unconditional love, bliss and peace.
- I am realizing my fullest potential.
- I am flowing with joy by divine will.
- I am living by being in the constant experience of who I truly am.

4. Be clear and precise (Exactly what)

A motivational trainer once asked his audience during a seminar, "How many of you want more money?"

Many participants raised their hands. The trainer handed out a ten-dollar bill to each one of them and asked, "You now have more money than before. Are you satisfied?"

They all smiled, "No, this won't suffice."

The trainer then handed out a hundred-dollar bill to each and asked, "Are you happy now?"

"No, we need a lot more!" came the reply

The coach explained, "How much is '*more*' for you? If I don't know how much you mean by *more*, how can I give it to you? In the same way, if you don't know how much money you want, how do you expect nature to arrange for it?!"

Most people want more of everything but they don't have a clear idea of how much '*more*' is. While writing the diary, write down in very precise terms about your wishes. Using the word 'more' in general, baffles the subconscious mind. Ask yourself, "What do I exactly want?"

Instead of: *I need to reduce my weight.*

Write: *My weight is …… kg on ……[date].*

Instead of: *I want more money* (or) *I want to be richer.*

Write: *I want Rs………. in my bank account by …………. [date/year].*

Instead of: *I want a better home.*

Write: *I want a penthouse with a terraced garden in ……. [locality].*

5. Write the Purpose of your Goal (Why)

In addition to writing your goals clearly, it is essential to write the purpose of your goal – the aim behind the goal.

Append the words "so that…" to your goal to state its purpose. Why? If a pessimistic thought ever occurs in your mind or in your speech, adding 'so that' can neutralize that thought or turn it into a positive one.

For example, instead of saying, "I want freedom" if you say, "I don't want bondage" then the latter would happen. Therefore, adding "so that…" is important. Now the same negative sentence would be, "I don't want bondage, *so that* I can enjoy freedom."

Adding "so that…" not only neutralizes the power of a negative thought, but also throws light on your core belief behind the negative thought. You can now try to make affirmative statements to otherwise seemingly negative thoughts or statements by adding "so that…". For instance, "I want to keep my child away from bad company, *so that* she grows up to become a respected and successful human being."

Adding "so that…" to a thought or a sentence forces you to deeply contemplate, which in turn helps in developing clarity about why you are demanding what you are. This helps in boosting confidence, bringing a feeling of happiness and enthusiasm. With this clarity, the seed of faith takes root and helps you in achieving your goal faster.

Here are some examples of how we can use "so that..." in our goal statements.

I want to gain complete health, *so that* I can take giant strides towards success in my chosen field.

I want a bigger car, *so that* I may bring comfort to my family.

I want a monthly salary of Rs........., *so that* I can take care of all my family needs, save Rs...... and also donate Rs...... to charity.

I want to imbibe the quality of patience in myself, *so that* I can experience peace in every situation.

I want to improve my relationships, *so that* I can feel joy and completeness in life.

I want to exercise regularly, *so that* my immune power improves.

I want to adopt healthy habits, *so that* I can attain the wealth of complete health.

6. Write in Present Tense (When)

What tense should we assume when we write the diary?

The answer to this question can vary from person to person, but it helps to choose the present tense. If we use the future tense, it goes into the subconscious mind as a future concept. The picture that is created deep within is that it is a future possibility, something that is not in the current reality.

On the other hand, it is empowering to state the goal in the present tense. Planting the idea that the desired state is already present, gives the subconscious mind the picture that the experience of the goal is present *right now*. This catalyzes the manifestation of the goal. Whatever you write, write it with faith in the present tense.

7. Read and Repeat with Faith

The next essential step is to read what you've written in the diary with faith. Mere writing is not enough, unless what you have written is reinforced through consistent repetition. Repeated reading will activate the seeds of faith. Soon the imagined state will become your reality.

Read out your goals three to four times a week; and read aloud if possible. Invest some time reflecting on them. Go through it with faith and a feeling of fulfilment. If possible, bring melody into your reading. Music, rhythm and tone are keys to access the subconscious mind.

Work on every individual goal by closing your eyes and imagining that you have already achieved it – feel it, visualize it, hear someone say it, see it coming in written form. Take a pause to feel what it is like to have achieved the goal. Let the feeling of joy and satisfaction sink in. Stay doused in this feeling for some time. This will also activate your willpower. It bridges the gap between your present and the imagined reality. By repeatedly reinforcing the belief that you have already achieved your goal, you help Nature manifest it in your life.

Manifest qualities, not things

Let us take a moment to understand what exactly do we want in life. What does every person exactly want? What does each one of us really want?

> When someone was asked what he wants, he said, "I want a smartphone."
>
> He was then asked, "Why do you want a smartphone?"
>
> He replied, "So that I can converse with people; so that I can get my tasks done."
>
> Further, he was asked, "Why do you want all this?"

He thought about it and then said, "That would make me happy."

When another person was asked the same question, he said, "I want to put an end to the daily quarrels that I have with my wife."

"Why do you want to put an end to it?"

"I wish for it to end so that my relationship with her improves."

"What will you gain by improving this relationship?"

He thought over this and replied, "Then I will experience love."

When someone else was asked what he wants, he answered, "I wish that the children in my neighbourhood stop playing in the common area after 8 p.m."

"Why?"

"Then I won't be troubled by the noise and commotion that they create."

"What will you gain with this?"

He replied, "I will be at peace."

We can see from these examples that when we delve deeper into man's desires, they finally amount to the experience of love, happiness and peace.

Try this out with yourself. Randomly choose any one wish that you have and ask yourself, "Why do I want this wish to be fulfilled? What will I really gain if the wish is fulfilled?" When you repeatedly question yourself this way, it will finally lead you to the seeking of either love, happiness, peace or a combination of these.

Now, it is a question worth asking that if each and every one of us is ultimately seeking Love, Bliss and Peace, then why are we all straying in diverse directions chasing our own individual desires? Think about it.

When we understand what we are actually looking for through all our endeavours, we find that we all want the same – "Love,

Happiness and Peace". This is the real desire of every human being and interestingly, love, peace and happiness are the very core qualities of who-we-truly-are. These qualities are inherent in our being. It's just that they have been shrouded behind a plethora of thoughts and desires.

When a person desires a good bank balance, his actual overarching desire is for peace and happiness stemming from abundance. He believes that peace would come from the assurance of having enough money and happiness from the comfort and luxuries that he can afford as a result of his wealth. So then, he should choose to manifest abundance, not just a good bank balance. The bank balance is already a part of the abundance.

Therefore, it is common sense to focus on the *qualities* that we wish to manifest, rather than material things. It is possible that someone who wished for a promotion could have become the owner of his own start-up company, had he only asked for *growth* instead of a promotion!

When we manifest higher qualities and they start expressing through us, everything else will automatically follow. It is about opening the mind, expanding our horizons and thinking bigger and higher!

Correct the Original Script of Life

The Faith Fair book can be developed as the blueprint for life. Suppose that we draw a picture and make photocopies of the same. If we were to find that there is something wrong with the picture, would you correct the original, or the photocopies? You would correct the original.

In the same way, if you find that situations occurring in life are not exactly as you would desire, what would you do? Would you correct the situations?

What you experience in the external world reflects what you hold within. The smart way is to make corrections in your inner world. You need to change the beliefs that constitute your faith within. The

Faith Fair book serves as a written energetic imprint of your original script for life.

Re-visit your Faith Fair book. See what you have written for the particular facet of life where this situation has occurred. If you haven't written anything at all, contemplate and write it down. If you've already written something, refine it.

At times, you may see things not happening as per your chosen goal and you may perhaps react in a fit of compulsion. But even under such circumstances, it helps to wait patiently with faith that whatever is written in the Faith Fair book is surely going to manifest!

6
PRINCIPLE 3
LIFE IS ON AUTOPILOT

A unit of soldiers that had recently been inducted into the army was undergoing pre-deployment training. The soldiers followed a very strict training regimen, dividing their time between physical training and the study of war procedures, surveillance, attack and defence strategies.

Strangely, except for a few, most of them were afraid of drowning for the lack of ability to swim. On the very first day of training, they had learned that there was no place for fear in a soldier's mind – whether for water, or for a bullet! And yet, even the thought of jumping into water would make many of them shudder.

One early morning, they left their training camp on their routine run. They chose a route that was different from the regular one. On this new route, the soldiers came across a wide river that had an old rickety bridge built across. The soldiers, who knew swimming did not hesitate, but the ones who didn't, were naturally afraid of crossing such an old and unreliable bridge.

With no other alternative and not wanting to invite their captain's wrath, they broke their run and began crossing the bridge, proceeding gingerly. The bridge – made of a few old wooden planks tied together – creaked louder with every step and the whole unit swayed frighteningly just a few feet above the gushing water. Just when the unit was close to the centre of the bridge, it finally gave way and the whole unit fell into the raging river.

The soldiers who knew swimming were able to swim with the water currents, but surprisingly even the ones who didn't know how to swim, somehow flapped their hands and kicked their legs in desperation and managed to touch the riverbank with the help of those who could swim.

Later, when the ones who didn't know how to swim were asked how they were able to pull of such a feat, almost all of them gave the same answer. "I just don't know how I did that! We couldn't save ourselves from falling into the water, but once we were in, our survival instinct got the better of our fear!"

A few months later, war broke out and all the infantry units – even the ones who had been freshly trained – had to be deployed on the warfront. This particular unit was assigned the task of destroying an enemy ammunition depot. When they embarked upon their mission, they came across a river that had to be crossed to reach the target. Since boats would be too big for crossing over, swimming was the only alternative. It was a do-or-die situation. Every soldier in the unit confidently jumped into the river and swam across. The unit accomplished its mission without any losses.

A few weeks after the war was won, the soldiers were discussing their experiences and realized something interesting. They remembered the day they had almost drowned due to the broken bridge. It was owing to that accident that the soldiers were able to overcome their fear of water and get the confidence to swim. Had the bridge not broken that day, they would never have been able to accomplish their mission and do their bit to serve their army.

This example is indeed relevant to our lives too; only the contexts change. We don't have control over situations in our lives. The way the soldiers didn't have any control over falling into the water, we too get drowned in the whirlpool of emotions over certain situations in our lives. These situations may seem negative at that given point, but in the context of the bigger picture, they are important stepping stones to a greater version of ourselves.

Every negative situation can serve as a reminder for us that our life is on autopilot, all the time being guided by Nature to fulfil our highest good. Life is designed to give us new skills and qualities to help us grow and realize our highest potential.

This is the third principle of faith – **Life is on autopilot. Trust it! Nature is always serving up your highest good.**

Let us try and understand what *"autopilot"* means in this context.

If a plane whose destination is Delhi is heading for a stopover at Mumbai, it doesn't mean that the plane is lost. It doesn't mean it is a failure of the flight. Mumbai is just a stopover en route to Delhi; a stepping stone, so to say. The final destination is Delhi and it will be reached. The passengers of the plane need to trust the pilot and the airline that they will get them to their destination. They need not give up in despair, thinking their journey is doomed.

Likewise, Nature's ways are often not straight and tangible. It knows what we need in our lives and fulfils our needs by bringing forth both good and bad situations. Our life is running on autopilot, being constantly guided by Nature.

When people make a wish, they expect its direct tangible manifestation. With such a mindset, if something apparently negative happens, or if results are not tangible, they immediately lose hope. We often view such situations with a negative perspective. This only makes the process slower and more fraught. Our actions and reactions constantly affect how soon our wishes are manifested.

If we greet the situations in life with a positive perspective, we indicate to Nature that we are constantly growing and understanding the lessons it is trying to teach us. On the other hand, if we resist the events in our lives and complain about them, we attract more of such scenarios in the future. Nature takes it as a sign of a 'need for further improvement' and keeps testing us until we grow to learn our lessons. These are vital lessons that help us develop great qualities like patience, acceptance, persistence, resilience and steadfastness.

Every situation is supposed to be a stepping stone, but we label it as happy or sad; positive or negative; good or bad and thus invite sorrow into our lives. In such a scenario, it helps to remember that life runs on autopilot mode and that we need to trust it to take us to the destination we've set for ourselves. We need to have faith in the autopilot and be assured that whatever we want is eventually and invariably going to come to us. What do we do in the meanwhile? We have to keep working on our faith, making it stronger than ever. We have to prepare ourselves to receive what comes. We have to enjoy the wait while it lasts!

Holding onto faith ensures our constant happiness as we accept every situation and learn to see the silver lining of every dark cloud in life. Life without faith is like holding an umbrella over our heads. When faced with a hard situation, we curse our luck, worrying why things have to happen to us. We pray for deliverance, not knowing that blessings are already raining down upon us every moment; all we need to do is do away with the umbrella! This umbrella is the umbrella of unnecessary fears and doubts that we unknowingly harbor. The situation is just a lesson. Faith helps us let go of this umbrella and enjoy the relentless flow of life.

> Bob worked at a software MNC as a development engineer. A 9-to-5 job, stable and good salary, good work-life balance, Saturday-night parties with colleagues; things were going fine for him when suddenly one fine day, Bob found himself talking to some staffing experts at his company.
>
> After a tense couple of weeks and some grueling interviews about what exactly Bob's minute-to-minute schedule at work was, he was laid off. It seemed to him that the world had come crashing down. His future plans, financial security, everything washed off in a single moment.
>
> The first day he spent at home, away from work, was a terribly depressing one. With nothing to do and no idea how to proceed in life, Bob was feeling extremely dejected. He began thinking, "What have I done to deserve this? I have always been hardworking, have attended church, made donations to charities,

been kind to the elderly and loving to the young! Why then am I a victim of such a fate?!"

Then one day, while Bob was standing in a queue at the mall to pay for groceries, he met an old college friend, Andy. Andy invited him for coffee. Not feeling like talking to anyone in the mindset that he was, Bob reluctantly agreed and the two talked about old days. The conversation drifted to the present and Bob told Andy about how badly he was placed. Andy, to Bob's surprise, had a very similar story to share about himself. "It's okay, Bob! We're smart people; we can think of something to do!" Andy assured him. Bob felt good after a long time, although he was fraught with doubts and fears.

Andy then went on to discuss a business opportunity with Bob. He told Bob how he had grown to have a very good rapport with one of his clients that he worked with at his previous job. After Andy lost his job, the client had approached him, offering him work as a consultant, as Andy knew the software in-and-out – having been one of the developers who had developed it in the first place. Andy had declined the offer then, thinking it would be too much work for a single person and had been doing odd jobs here and there, ever since.

Now that he had met Bob, who was just as good a developer as he was, he proposed the idea of approaching the client together and finding out if the opportunity was still open. Having nothing better to do, Bob agreed. Fortunately, the opportunity was still open and soon they rented a little office and began working with this client. The days of distress that both of them had endured, made them both exceptionally hardworking and the client was all praises for them.

One happy client led to another and they were soon serving many more clients, enough for them to plan to move to a bigger office and hire a large staff. Sitting in a small but cozy cabin one fine day, Bob was looking out of the window, reminiscing the days that had gone by and realizing how getting fired from his job had turned out to be such a great blessing!

People find it difficult to have faith in the unseen. Before Bob met Andy and began his start-up, if he were told that getting fired from his job was actually a blessing, he would never have believed!

When people say "Whatever happens, happens for the good", it is faith that they place in positivity. The situations may be adverse and the total opposite of what you desire, but the faith remains steadfast – that is the key to success. Had Bob the same unfaltering faith, he wouldn't have endured so much sorrow and self-doubt.

Whatever happens is for the best

> Some fishermen had taken their boats into waters to catch their batch of fish. After a while, it started raining heavily. It was a heavy and unrelenting downpour; bolts of lightning filled the sky. The wind blew furiously. The fishermen's boats swayed about dangerously and were in the risk of drowning. The ocean waves joined in the cacophony and chaos, displacing the boats. The fishermen tried very hard to steer their boats and maintain direction, but it seemed almost impossible in the storm.
>
> After an hour or two, the storms calmed down. The fishermen were thankful to be alive. But, the next challenge facing them was finding their way home to the coast. They had no idea where they were, how far into the ocean or which direction they had drifted. They tried going ahead small distances in different directions but to no avail.
>
> The fishermen had almost lost hope of ever going back home when they saw a flicker of light in the dark expanse around them. They were overjoyed! Light meant warmth and life – and more than anything else, it probably meant land! They followed the expanding speck of light, which led them to the shore.
>
> Upon finally reaching their village, they were astonished to find that the life-saving light was in fact a huge fire which was consuming the fishermen's village because of the bolts of lightning. The fire was dealt with soon enough and the fishermen were reunited with their families.

One of the fishermen's wife came running to him crying that their house was gutted down in the raging fire. But, instead of despair, his face showed signs of relief and happiness. He explained to his wife that the fire may have burnt down their house, but it had also saved his life! The fisherman's wife was struck by this new perspective.

She realized that Nature had set the entire plan. Suddenly, the destructive fire that had burned down their village, which had seemed a very bad thing, now turned out to have been a blessing in disguise! It brought a new perspective to the situation. Everything in the world – whether negative or positive – has a constructive role to play.

Seeing the entire picture clearly in hindsight, it becomes easy for us to infer that whatever Nature does is for the best. However, it is only when we have faith in this truth *before* situations unfold, that we can accept both the positive and negative experiences as stepping stones. This realization is important. It is easy to be convinced by hindsight. But, we tend to lose faith in Nature when we are in a particular situation. In such instances, our faith can gain a boost if we remind ourselves that "*This is not the complete picture; my life is on autopilot and whatever is happening is for my best!*"

This principle of faith can also be stated as – **Nature is always serving up your highest good**.

It is easy to say and accept that whatever happens, happens for the best when the context is a positive and favorable incident, situation or circumstance. However, the same understanding seems all the more difficult to apply if something untoward or undesirable happens. This just doesn't seem to fit the logic! We need to remind ourselves that this is only the first half of the Divine Plan of Nature. It may seem challenging and we tend to withdraw because the latter part is not yet visible to us. The challenge lies in keeping a steadfast faith even in the unfavorable part of the Divine plan.

Take the example of a person, who has just met with an accident. On the face of it, this would be perceived as an undesirable situation that caused only pain and distress. However, upon contemplation, we will find that some positivity – however miniscule – outlines this seemingly negative incident. One reason why we are not able to perceive things positively is because we have a very rigidly programmed and reinforced idea of what is positive and what is not.

Anything that we desire is positive and that which we don't is negative. This is a very clear line we inadvertently draw in our minds. What we fail to understand is that when we deem something as negative or positive, we do it based on our limited intelligence and shortsightedness. Consequently, something that we perceive as good or bad for ourselves, is not necessarily so.

It is possible that the person, who had the accident, had been intending to take a break from work for rest but was not able to. The accident gave him that pretext and the opportunity to take that long awaited break. It is also possible that he may not have spent time with his family, and the rest that follows the accident gives him an opportunity to slow down and spend time with them. The accident may make him a cautious and careful driver and hence avert an even bigger, more critical accident in the future.

These are just a few examples of seeing the positive outcome of a negative incident. There will surely be more if one cares to contemplate upon it. Even if people believe that Nature goes wrong at times, it is not true. Nature never goes wrong and it makes no mistakes. It is not always possible to comprehend how Nature is always serving up our highest good. Hence, it is vital that we develop unquestionable faith in the unseen ways of Nature.

It is faith which ensures our endurance as we travel the journey by Nature's plan. It is faith which helps us see the miracle in every situation and helps us in being receptive to the providence of Nature. It is faith that helps us see that Nature is always guiding us as we autopilot through life! If we are able to believe that whatever happens, happens for the best, *after* the complete picture has unfolded, why not have faith in this truth *before* the picture unfolds?!

Whatever has happened, is happening and will happen, will all be for the best!

Nature serves Challenges to bring out Your Best

> Suppose a little child wants to play cricket but has no one to play with. He insists that his father should play with him. The father is not very interested, but he loves his child and doesn't want to dishearten him. So, he agrees.
>
> The child prefers to bat and improve his game, so that he can be selected for his school team. What does the father do? Of course, he will bowl, so that his darling child can practice batting! Not that he likes to bowl, but he would still do it out of love for his child.
>
> Now, the father would love to see him improve his game and be selected for higher league matches. What does he do? He bowls bouncers and googlies (deceptive spinning balls) at his child. The child feels let down when he is unable to face the ball effectively and protests that his father is unfair. He even complains that his father does not love him, and hence is making batting difficult for him.
>
> The father then explains to his child lovingly that he is raising the difficulty level of the game, only so that his son can become an expert at the game and hit the ball out of the ground with confidence, without being flustered by googlies or bouncers. He teaches his son to read the bowling carefully so that he can hit the bouncers and googlies for sixes and fours.
>
> When the child learns the art of getting on top of the bowling and batting with poise and confidence, he feels grateful for his father's contribution in his success.

In the game of cricket, you need someone to bowl to you so that you can enjoy batting. Without bowlers, you can never get to bat and you won't be able to mature into an ace batsman. This metaphorical game of cricket between the father and the child resembles the game of life. The father here represents your relationships – your family, friends, neighbors, colleagues, managers, subordinates, your local civic services and also the government!

People around you are partners, contributors, co-creators in the journey of your life.

All these people, who play a variety of roles in your daily life, avail you the opportunity to mature and develop vital qualities like patience, unconditional love, faith, playfulness, consistency, resilience, courage, steadfastness, communication to name a few. It is only when you develop these higher qualities that you truly grow and mature and bring about a transformation within and around you.

The reality is, we're here to grow – physically, mentally, emotionally and spiritually. When growth stops, we automatically feel stagnant and dull. Without growth, we aren't fulfilling the purpose of being here on earth in this human form. We are all work in progress!

When do your best qualities get a chance to manifest?

When valleys are deep, the hills appear equally high. When people bowl bouncers at you, you have a chance of scoring runs. The one who wants to become an expert at this game of life doesn't fear the bouncers of setbacks or difficult situations. He knows that these are opportunities to score well in the game of life. When someone helps you in a way that's obvious, you feel that they wish you well. However, when someone puts you down or constrains your progress, you may feel they are being unfair by bowling real-life bouncers and googlies at you. But consider that the worst behavior of others is meant for bringing out the best in you. Nature is serving you challenges to help you grow.

When we feel disheartened when others don't support us in testing times, we need to have faith that by not supporting, they are actually helping us in evolving into a better version of ourselves.

It is never too late to have faith

Fables may be simple bed-time stories with morals for kids that feature animals and birds. But they sometimes also carry very important life lessons for grown-ups too. Here's one such fable that will help us understand a very important aspect of faith.

> Somewhere far off in a forest, there was a pregnant deer, who was desperately looking for a decent place, where she could give birth to her fawn. After looking high and low, she finally saw a pile of dry grass that looked safe and warm on the bank of a river. As she settled into the grass, she began having the initial labor pains.
>
> Just then, clouds filled the sky and bolts of lightning began to lash out. One such lightning struck the ground near the pile of grass and the dry tinder instantly caught fire. The wind had already picked up by now and the fire rapidly spread across the field to the neighboring trees. The forest in the vicinity was now ablaze. The deer's pains were intensifying. Not knowing what to do, she looked around to see where she could go. To her great anguish, she noticed a hunter to her right pointing an arrow pointer at her, ready to release it any moment. To her left, she noticed a lion moving towards her, ready to pounce any moment.
>
> It was indeed a critical situation – a hunter to her right, ready to kill her; a hungry lion to her left, ready to devour her; a raging fire around her in the forest, a wildly turbulent river in front of her that couldn't be crossed.
>
> What could the deer do at that moment? Would she be able to give birth to the fawn? If so, would she and the fawn survive? Would she be the victim of the fatal arrow shot by the hunter? Would she be killed at the hands of the lion? Or would she be drowned in trying to cross the river?
>
> Take a moment to step into the story and consider what you would have done in the deer's place. Consider your options and the risks. Add anything else that you think necessary to evaluate the situation. And do not forget to factor in the panic that is naturally felt in such a dire situation!

Read on to find out what happened...

The deer realized her desperate situation. She fathomed that there was nowhere else she could go and nothing she could do to improve the situation. Finally, she decided to pray with deep faith.

"I am *deer* of God," she prayed with all her intensity, "and nothing but Faith can *touch* me!"

She repeated these words with all the sincerity in her heart, knowing that if she would be delivered from her situation, this was the only way. To her surprise, as she repeated these words, a strange calmness came over her and she felt the warmth of courage. She even smiled at the pun in her prayer! She ignored everything around her and just focused on giving birth to her little one – to make her little one's entry into this wonderful world as smooth and comfortable as she could.

She chose to focus on life and ignore all the symptoms of death around her. She tried to settle down again.

Just then, in a single instant, a lot of things happened...

A bolt of lightning struck the ground near the hunter making him jump. The surprised hunter lost his aim, released the arrow and ran away, frightened that he'd be burnt. The arrow zipped past the deer and struck the lion, killing him instantly. The thunderstorms lashed down over the forest and doused the fire. The very next moment, the deer gave birth to a healthy fawn.

The story has a simple but profound lesson – **It is never too late to have faith**. However desperate, critical or dire the situation may be, know that when there is nothing left to do, it is still a good time to begin to have faith. If there remains nothing to do in the outer physical world, one can turn inwards and pray. Pray in spite of the feelings of fear and panic because prayer in itself is the answer to the situation –

"I am dear of God; only faith can touch me; my safety and success are assured"

When we pray thus, when we decide to have faith, we attune ourselves to God; to Nature. And with the all-knowing nature guiding us, we know nothing can go wrong!

However negative or helpless our situation may appear today, we can remind ourselves that it is not too late to have faith; that whatever is happening is for the greater good and that whatever it is that we dearly wish is eventually going to come to us.

Thomas Edison, the inventor of the electric bulb, failed countless times at his attempts to make it work before he eventually succeeded. His invention wasn't a single stroke of success. He had to be resilient and perseverant. Imagine the dejection he must have felt each time his experiment failed! His lab even caught fire, burning down his equipment and notes. Think of what kept him going? It is true that he was resilient, but what fueled his resilience?

Faith. A deep conviction that he would achieve his goal someday.

Later, when he was interviewed, he is known to have said, "I haven't failed. I have just found 10,000 ways that it won't work!" This translates into the fact that every time he failed, it was a step closer to his goal; or at least that was the way he saw it. Every failure was in fact a guidance from Nature that that particular way wasn't the right one, followed by a newer and better idea.

This is also a great illustration of how the faith of a single person led to the betterment of the entire human race that followed, to this day! The world is filled with such inspiring examples of people, who have overcome impossible challenges, achieved impossible feats, defeated desperate situations and done miraculous feats, all of that with just the power of faith!

7

PRINCIPLE 4

THE HIGHEST FORM OF FAITH

Faith is inherent in every human being. It's just that it is expressed in various degrees in various people. When someone is in a difficulty, others tell them, "Just have faith; it will work out." It evokes the feeling of assurance within and the person feels empowered to overcome the difficulty.

People develop faith in their friends, in well-wishers, in parents, in themselves, in their own qualities and capabilities or simply in the art of staying optimistic and positive.

Little children tend to have unquestionable faith in their parents. They trust them and believe everything they are told. When their parents toss them up in the air, they do not panic because they are assured that their parents will catch them safely. Little children trust the waves like they trust the shore, only because of such unswerving faith.

Children then learn to have faith in teachers. As they grow into adolescence, they begin to develop faith in whom they idolize – celebrities and friends. They believe their words and follow their actions. They mimic the thinking and behavior of their idols.

Youngsters develop numerous beliefs, false or otherwise, due to their faith in friends and even on social media. They value attention and admiration gained on social media and begin to act in ways that are considered "cool", showing off an "attitude", gathering "likes" and so on.

Thus, throughout life, our faith keeps changing. People feel good even when they express faith in material things or superficial relationships. Such faith does help them to some extent in overcoming difficulties and achieving personal milestones in life.

Imagine what we can achieve if our faith were to evolve to a stature that is purer and higher!

A Higher form of Faith

A purer and higher form of faith is faith in God. When we mention God, it may draw out various ideas and pictures that each one holds within them. God, in the context of our discussion, does not carry a religious connotation as in being a product of any particular religious belief. God transcends religion; God represents the ultimate reality that is the foundation of all religions.

God refers to the Universal Consciousness, the True Self, Divine Intelligence, or the Essence of life. In simple terms, we may even call it Nature, the Universe or anything that you believe to hold the ultimate power. When someone has this faith, he considers God as the most powerful entity in the universe that can help him achieve the things he wants. Those who have this faith, pray to God, visit temples, shrines, or holy places and firmly believe that God will deliver what they have prayed for. And many a times, this faith indeed comes to fruition and people do achieve what they desire.

But although faith in God is a purer and higher form of faith, it is still not the pinnacle of faith. Be it faith in God or faith in your friends or relatives, such faith assumes that we are a body-mind—a limited individual being. If we remain stuck with this identity of ourselves, we can express faith only to the extent that fulfils the needs and desires of the body-mind alone. And this brings about limited results.

If we consider ourselves to be our body-mind, we remain trapped in individual personal desires that engulf us in the cycle of pain and pleasure. Is this the purpose of human life? Surely, human life can rise to a stature that transcends the individual.

Human life can attain the height of faith, joy, freedom, love and peace. However, rare are such souls as the Buddha, Adi Shankaracharya, Jesus, Prophet Muhammad, Saint Kabir and other self-realized masters who could experience such height of faith. It was possible for them because they had awakened to the truth that they were not limited to their body-minds, but were unlimited beings! These enlightened souls could express the ultimate faith of who they truly were.

It is a common belief that God created man, and most people live with this belief. But it is rare to experience the truth that **God did not create man; God *became* man**. Faith in this truth is the ultimate form of faith. This faith can be called **Faith *of* God**, **not faith *in* God**.

The Highest form of Faith

Faith *of* God refers to the faith that God had while creating this phenomenal world. What was the faith of God? God created the world with the faith that His creations would be a medium for Him to experience Himself and express His great qualities and possibilities.

He assumes innumerable forms with the desire to experience Himself, His vast potential, through every possible creation. This is exactly like an ocean taking the form of a wave—that emerges from the ocean and dissolves into the ocean. Since the wave has emerged from the ocean, it has no individual existence without the ocean. Each wave is the ocean itself; it is not something separate from the ocean. If you study a wave, you will find that the wave is nothing but the ocean. The properties of the wave are the same in essence as the ocean. It's just that the ocean endlessly takes the shape of waves. Waves arise and fall, but the ocean constantly exists as the waves and expresses through the waves!

Although God experiences Himself through various other forms like animals, birds, trees, etc., He donned the human form to consciously know Himself as the Essence of all, to be aware of Himself as the Being that lives through all forms. This possibility does not exist in other forms, where the experience of *being* is present unconsciously.

It is through the human form alone that God forgets Himself and then rejoices in re-remembering His divine truth as the life of everything. The operator of each one of our bodies is none else but God, and this is also our true identity. Each one of us is God in essence. Our lives are the expression of admiration, appreciation and joy of our own creation. Our lives are the expression of divine qualities – faith being one of them. We are here with our bodies to enjoy the divine game of life that the Creator is playing with Himself.

So, are the drops of the ocean separate from one another? Are they separate from the ocean? Not in essence. They are just different expressions of the same ocean. Therefore, it is just an illusion that we all are separate from each other and from our true Self. The five fingers of our hand are all different. Yet, the little finger does not grumble about its size and lead a sad life. Neither does the middle finger develop an ego that it is the tallest. All five fingers belong to the hand, performing different functions in unison, and it is the body that is experiencing various experiences with the help of the five fingers. The fingers are just the medium; the real experiencer is the body.

In the same way, while each individual "body-mind" is different due to the personality that it dons, the ultimate experiencer is only one. The body-mind mechanism is merely the medium through which the true Self experiences and expresses itself. Who is actually experiencing the world through us? When we ask these profound questions, we recall our true Self.

Imagine the joy when we realize through experience that we are the universal Self that is more grand and divine than what we had assumed ourselves to be—the limited separate individual! This is what Self-realization is all about – getting to know our real nature, our true identity. If you have faith that you are one with the universal Self and express it, you gain complete fulfilment in life. The expression of this ultimate faith comes along with bliss.

Today, many people mistakenly believe spirituality as performing rites, rituals and worship or reading the scriptures. Such activities are reminders or pointers to spirituality. They may help in releasing faith *in* God. However, one has to rise above this understanding and lead life with the faith *of* God. Then there are people who lead their lives blindfolded by the false belief that they don't need spirituality. They too need to understand and express the ultimate faith, viz. spiritual faith.

Expressing the Ultimate Faith

Having Faith *of* God implies understanding that *whatever is true for God is true for us*. The 'God' we refer to here is not a man-made God that we have been seeing on TV or movies. In this book, the name 'God' is used with the purpose of convenience. Here 'God' refers to the Formless essence of all creation. It is the Source of love, joy, peace and creativity. It is the living principle that pervades everyone and everything. It is that which is eternal and nameless, yet, each one of us is blessed with a free will to name the Ultimate Truth in a way that helps us to raise our faith.

How does the ocean see the wave? It sees it as its own expression. It sees it with the same possibilities that are inherent in the ocean itself. Similarly, God or the Universal Consciousness sees its individual expressions as being filled with divine qualities and magnificent possibilities. And how does the wave see itself? The wave thinks, "I am so little… I am insignificant… I have less than others." The wave cannot express its faith to the fullest until someone reminds it of its true nature. With this analogy of the wave, we too are being reminded of our grand nature.

So, are we considering ourselves as helpless, poor or weak waves that are victims of life situations? Is this how God or your Higher Self regards us? Not at all! This is what God intends to communicate to us. Whenever we get caught up in the web of negative thoughts, God instantly sends us a message in the form of a bad feeling. This is how God communicates with us that He doesn't think this way about us. God knows that what we think about ourselves is not our true nature. He reminds us of this truth, "You are made in My image… You are part of Me… You are essentially one with Me… You *are* Me. You have the same potential and power as I do." However, most of us rarely listen to His voice. Rather, we do not realize that God communicates with us through the language of feelings.

The fourth principle of faith states that: **When we consciously express the *Faith of God* in words, it brings us into alignment with our divine nature and unfolds our highest potential.**

Thus, whenever you feel self-pity and other associated negative feelings, remind yourself to welcome Godly or Divine thoughts. Ask yourself, "How does God see me? Helpless…? Worthless…? Someone with a low-profile…? Weak or ill…?" Of course not! God never sees anybody this way. Instead, God has a grander vision about you; he has a divine plan brimming with love, joy, peace and abundance working for you.

The negative feelings that we experience are actually a springboard to jump higher, it is a push from God to break the limitations of the mind and fly high. Otherwise, when we are stuck in our comfort-zone, we don't make an effort to take the leap of faith until nature pushes us with these negative feelings. It is when we get tired of negative feelings that we decide to break through self-imposed limitations to evolve and progress.

8
THE VOICE OF FAITH

Everyone would love to lead a life of constant happiness. But this depends on whether we are living the life that we were meant to.

Imagine an artist who paints the picture of a paintbrush. This is no ordinary picture of a paintbrush. This paintbrush comes alive inside the painting and serves to create more paintings *for the artist*. However, what if the paintbrush were to *assume* its own individual existence and a separate personal purpose? It would go about painting without consulting the artist. Though it was created to explore and express the artist's creative inspiration, the paintbrush will do something else without seeking to fulfill the artist's wish.

In much the same way, the human body-mind mechanism is meant to serve the manifestation of the *Creator's* creative inspiration. However, human beings perceive life from a limited personalized standpoint and function as individuals. Though a lot of individual and group creations may be happening in the visible realm, they are devoid of lasting contentment as the Creator's purpose remains unfulfilled.

Let us understand this with the help of an analogy. Consider a sheet of paper on which letters of the alphabet are written. Each written letter contributes to the story that the author wishes to write. However, if any single letter were to decide to express itself differently, then will the story flow as the author intended? If a single letter were to look around the sheet and compare itself with the other letters, it may find some letters that are bigger in size, some that are in beautiful italics, some are bolded and hence standout. This letter may then feel dejected by comparing thus and wish that it should be like or even better than the others. It could lose faith in its own original ability. However, unless the letter attains the perspective of the author or surrenders to his will, the very purpose of why it was penned on the paper is lost.

If we draw a parallel to human life, we see that individual human life is an expression on the stage of life, contributing to the overall plan of the creator. As Shakespeare has said, *"All the world's a stage; and all the men and women merely players; they have their exits and their entrances."* If any person gets into the game of comparison and the need for superiority and enacts such tendencies, it becomes an abnormality, a deviation from the grand plan of the creator.

We can manifest the Creator's plan only when the first creation happens first. The first creation is the act of seeking inspiration from the creator within by accessing the inner silence that exists in the background of our mind. This is essential to play our part; only then can we experience true fulfilment.

When we align with the true Self within us, we live the life we were meant to and we feel fulfilled and happy. When we are not aligned, we feel lost and at loggerheads with life. To be aligned with the true Self, we need to follow our Heart. The Heart does not mean the physical heart, but rather the inner seat of being. It is where our existence can be felt – beyond thoughts and emotions. It is from this very core that we receive inspiration.

When we connect with the Heart, we're happy and peaceful. When we are in that state, nothing can shake us. Some people refer to this as "being in the zone"; others call this "serenity' – beyond the highs and lows of pleasure and pain. This natural state is the experience of pure consciousness – beyond thoughts. It is the simple and yet profound experience of being alive.

This experience of being alive is continuously going on within every human being. It is felt as the constant sense of presence that goes on in the background of daily life events. When we rest in this experience, we open ourselves to inspiration. If we are unable to experience this natural state of being in our everyday humdrum, it is because it is veiled by the constant noise of thoughts in the head.

Being aligned with the Heart is the key to joy, peace and harmony with life. Distrusting the Heart blocks joy and peace. Following the Heart is the most important thing you can do, because it is ONLY this that can give you true fulfilment.

Noise of the Ego

The trouble is that we are habituated to listen to our thoughts in the head; so we cannot hear what our Heart says; and these thoughts are often at odds with our Heart. We listen to our thoughts instead of seeking inspiration from the Heart. Our thoughts— the ongoing commentary in our head— come from the ego – from the notion of being a separate limited individual. Inspiration of the Heart arises from the true Self – from pure consciousness.

The thoughts of the ego are filled with comparison, judgment, labelling things as 'good' or 'bad'. These thoughts arise from our past conditioning, our mind's programming that has happened since childhood. We believe that these are our thoughts. But they actually belong to the conditioned self-image – the ego or "false self".

The conditioning of the mind is just a collection of beliefs and information, and this is what makes up the ego. So, the ego makes our life decisions based on these beliefs and information. It cannot provide guidance about how to lead our life. Negative memories have a lasting impact on conditioning our responses to life situations. If we are cut off from our Heart, then we are left with such conditioned thoughts to guide us.

When we are identified with this conditioning, we feel discontent. We experience distrust, fear and insecurity, which we try to overcome by acquiring comforts, possessions, money, status, power, and control. We remain identified with the conditioning of the ego due to its thoughts of fear, doubts and distrust. The ego does not trust life, and it convinces us that life cannot be trusted; that anything can go wrong; and we end up trusting such thoughts of the ego. We can never have faith in life if we trust the thoughts that stem from the ego. To be able to truly have faith on life, we first have to clearly see and be convinced that the ego cannot be trusted.

Aligning with the Heart

While the ego functions from incompleteness and discontent, the heart exudes peace and contentment. The Heart is where we connect with the Source of all creation. Thoughts that arise from the Heart are inherently impersonal in nature. They are not centred on an individual person; they serve the larger good of all and are an expression of divine qualities like love, joy, peace, compassion, trust, gratitude, creativity and faith.

The Heart is the source of wisdom and it communicates through inspiration, through intuition and insight, that manifest as feelings, visuals, or words. The Heart directs us towards finding true fulfilment.

How do we shift from an ego-driven living towards alignment with the Heart?

For this, we need to observe the play of the ego for what it truly is. We need to notice how the thoughts of the ego go 'hyper' by judging and painting situations in extreme ways. We need to be vigilant about the conditioned responses that arise from the head and use them as opportunities to dip into the heart.

The other important step is to elevate our faith in life, to begin trusting the Heart. This can be done by opening ourselves to thoughts of divine inspiration. Verbalizing such thoughts helps in steering clear from the noise of the ego and aligning with the Voice of Faith.

The Voice of Faith

Our lives can be transformed if we consciously lend our voice to thoughts of Divine inspiration that arise from the Heart. These can be called Divine thoughts for the purpose of this discussion. As soon as we express even one such Divine thought, we get a good feeling as it raises our level of consciousness. With this elevated consciousness, we can witness that the so-called problems or challenges that we face begin to dissolve.

Choose to give voice to Divine thoughts. Let divine words flow in your speech. This is the Voice of Faith. Faith in this case indicates that you believe in your divinity; that you have total conviction that you are the Universal, All-Powerful Self, and therefore when you utter something, it has to come true. The Voice of Faith is thus a magic potion that you don't have to take in, but rather produce (express) with your tongue. Always remember: WHAT IS TRUE FOR GOD, IS TRUE FOR ME.

What faith has God placed in creating this Universe? And what is the faith of God in creating human life? If we understand the faith that God has placed in human life, then how would we lead our lives? Do we have faith in the faith that God has placed on us? These are profound questions that need to be contemplated.

Are we leading a life of struggle, being disturbed and despondent about the slightest happenings in life? Are we complaining or blaming people or the stars for what we perceive as our life situations? If we can grasp even an iota of measure of the grandeur that God envisions in us, our lives would be rid of all negativity and limitations. When we muster the courage to place our faith on the faith that God has placed on us, we will then gain confidence about leading life based on faith in the unseen.

If you are feeling unhappy or upset about something, ask yourself what would God say about unhappiness. He would probably say, "I have made man in my image to experience bliss and express boundless joy. I AM THE SOURCE OF JOY." To express faith, feel this and speak it out mentally or loudly. As soon as you use the Voice of Faith, you will be able to shift your vibration back to your True Self. You will be able to detach yourself from ongoing situations.

If you are feeling hatred or contempt, if you are feeling unloved or lonely, lend your voice to God's thoughts, "I have made man in my image to experience love and express love and compassion. This world is an expression of unconditional love. I AM THE SOURCE OF LOVE." Speak this out and allow love to permeate your heart.

If you are feeling restless, irritated or angry, speak God's thoughts: "I have made man in my image to experience and express peace. I AM THE SOURCE OF PEACE."

If you are feeling low on self-esteem, proclaim your divinity, "Man is My (God's) descendant. I am limitless, all-knowing and all-pervading."

In the facet of health, proclaim what God would proclaim about the human embodiment and lend your Voice of Faith— "I have created man and his body in my image. It is whole and perfect. Let the human body serve as the expression of pure consciousness."

When we realize our true identity as pure consciousness beyond the body and mind, when we realize our oneness with the Creative principle, then we can voice our faith in who we truly are.

It helps to consciously repeat the following lines with faith and passion.

- I am one with God.
- I am made in the image of God.
- This body-mind is an expression of the Creator.
- What is true for God is true for Me.
- What is possible for God is possible for Me.

- I am Love; I am Bliss; I am Peace; I am Completeness.
- I am free; I am freedom.
- I am pure; I am the divine state of Enlightenment.
- My body and mind are becoming the perfect medium for experiencing who-I-truly-am and expressing my limitless potential.
- I am health; my body-mind is becoming the perfect expression of health and vitality.

Expressing the Voice of Faith is not a form of affirmation, nor is it an attempt to change your self-talk. It is about having faith in the highest possibility and verbalizing what the Source would want to. Continue producing the magic potion of the Voice of Faith through your speech until you reach the ultimate state of being—freedom from the sense of individuality and becoming who-you-actually-are—the Supreme Self. Then, you won't need to say anything, you will just *be*.

The Voice of Faith will remind you of your true self—the source of love, joy, peace, health and prosperity. However, having read so far, many do think, "No, this cannot be true. If I am not feeling any love, how can I say that I am love? Does this not amount to lying?" This question can be best answered with the help of a story.

> A thief, running from the police, sneaked into a temple priest's house. The priest saw him and treated him like a guest. He let him stay in his house for a few days. Before leaving, the thief stole a gold lamp that was lying in the worship hall.
>
> A few days later, the thief was caught and the police found the gold lamp in his possession. Their investigation led them to the priest. When they asked the priest if the lamp belonged to him, the priest replied, "I had gifted this lamp to this man. He was my guest for a few days." Since the police could not find any other evidence against the thief, they let him go.

The thief turned to the priest and expressed his gratitude, "Thank you for saving me; I would have been behind bars if it was not for you. But why did you lie, being a priest!?"

The priest replied, "I lied because I have full faith that *this is your last theft.*"

The thief got the jolt of his life. It was for the first time that someone had placed such faith on him. Indeed, he did stop stealing and mended his ways. The priest's Voice of Faith won, even though it may have seemed like a lie.

The Voice of Faith is never a lie. It expresses faith in the unseen, in the higher possibility. It is the expression of faith in something that is yet to manifest in physical form. Even if it seems a lie, the deep assurance that is held in faith has the power to turn the tables on the situations that bother you. When we repeat the above lines of faith, it eventually has to work, because we are stating the truth of who-we-truly-are. We are lending our voice to invoke our true potential, which is only shrouded by our beliefs.

So, what did the priest do? He transformed the theft into faith and indeed it turned out to be the thief's last theft. The faith of the priest brought about a miracle. Through his faith, the priest invoked the highest possibility from the incident of theft.

Consider what would have happened if the priest had handed over the thief over to the police? The thief would have continued with his inappropriate ways in life. He wouldn't have got the opportunity to change and mend his ways. The priest was aligned with the Heart – he was open to divine inspiration and thus he was able to make such an uncommon choice in the scenario. It is only when one is at an elevated level of faith that such choices can emerge.

This is the power of faith. People go to great lengths to release their faith. They perform penance; they visit holy shrines, walking long distances by foot; they perform elaborate rituals as instructed by priests, and so on. But this faith can be released wherever you are, provided you are aligned with the Heart. All you need to do is start voicing your faith in Divine thoughts.

Let the Voice of Faith permeate every cell of your body. Like you interweave threads of wool to make a sweater, interweave the voice of faith with every cell of your body. Knit it so closely that it never comes off or loosens. Let faith in Divine thoughts become your nature. Verbalize Divine thoughts about happiness, abundance, love, peace, etc.

9

PRINCIPLE 5
BETRAYAL IS A MYTH, FAITH THE TRUTH

Experience the tranquility that comes from faith. Experience what it means to "let go". The situation that you're trying to resolve is already being worked upon by Nature long before you did and in a better way beyond human comprehension! So be thankful instead of being anxious.

Counteract Betrayal with Faith-inspired Actions

There was a hunter, who had lost his way in the forest. After wandering in different directions for a long time, when dusk finally started to settle, he decided to take refuge on a tree for the night and try to find his way out in the morning.

He walked around a bit to find a big tree with a lot of foliage so that he could save himself from the rain, for it had started to get cloudy as well. The cries of wild animals and noise of insects filled the night. Barks, howls and roars seemed even more terrifying when accompanied by the thunderbolts, stirring the fear in his mind.

Finally, as the last rays of sunlight withdrew from the sky, he found a tree that he thought would keep him safe. Just as he was studying the tree to find a place where he could start climbing, he got the uncomfortable feeling that he was not alone. He slowly looked around to see what it was when he suddenly confronted his worst fear! A lion was standing a few meters away from him, staring at him!

The hunter instinctively ran towards the tree and grabbed it in a desperate attempt to climb. For the next few seconds, all he did was to grab whatever came to his hands to get as far away from the lion and as higher up the tree as possible. Every now and then he would hear the lion roar as it tried to reach for his feet to pull him down. A few minutes later, when he was convinced that he was out of the reach of the lion, he took a look around him to find a place to sit, for his legs were aching badly from his climb.

He realized for the first time that whatever his hands were holding, was too furry and soft to be a tree branch! He looked closely and what did he see?! He was holding the legs of a bear! The branch that he had climbed onto, was already occupied by a bear!

"This is it!" the hunter thought, "I saved myself from the lion only to be devoured by a bear!" A lion below, a bear in the front and nowhere to go! His legs went limp. He started to tremble all over and even though the night was cold, beads of sweat rolled down his forehead. He was staring at his death.

Just then, sensing the hunter's fear, the bear spoke, "Do not fear me. You seek shelter in my home and you shall find it here. Trust me, I shall keep you safe from the lion." These words seemed almost unbelievably true to the hunter! Feelings were mixed. On the one hand, he doubted the bear's intent; on the other hand, he was tearfully overwhelmed by gratitude. Finally, deciding that there was no other option, the hunter thanked the bear and settled onto the branch.

The lion overheard their conversation and roared in anger, "I'm not going anywhere. We shall see whose patience lasts longer!" The lion sat down right under the branch on which the hunter and the bear were perched.

Hours went by and the lion still showed no signs of moving away. As the night grew darker, the hunter started feeling sleepy. The bear was yawning too. Feeling desperately hungry, the lion told the bear, "How long are you going to help this human? He is falling asleep, just give him a nudge so that he falls down and we can eat him together. I promise, you will have your fair share… I am sure you are hungry as well."

The hunter heard the lion's words and felt his stomach churn. He felt certain that the bear would accept his proposal and throw him down the tree. However, the bear sternly replied, "He has taken refuge with me. He has trusted me; I shall not betray him." The hunter breathed a sigh of relief and the lion kicked the ground in frustration. He was left with no alternative but to wait.

A little later, the bear dozed off on one of the branches while the hunter stayed awake out of fear. The lion saw that the bear was asleep and now tried to lure the hunter, "It doesn't matter to me whom I eat as long as I get something to eat. How long are you going to stay perched up on a tree? Nudge the bear off the branch and you shall go home safely. I'm surely going to kill one of you tonight; don't you want to be the one to live tomorrow morning?"

A selfish greed to stay alive creeped within the hunter. "How long is the bear going to protect me?" he thought, "Let me just push him off the tree and finish the matter once and for all. I can then go home safely! He is asleep anyway; it will all be over even before he realizes what's happening." The hunter decided to accept the lion's proposal and pushed the bear off the branch. The bear was in deep sleep and did not realize what was happening. As he came crashing down, one of his paws got stuck in one of the branches and it saved him from falling. The bear quickly came to his senses and climbed back up the tree.

The hunter saw the whole incident. He now felt that he had betrayed the bear; there was no way he was going to let him off alive. The bear would surely throw him down to the lion. However, the bear did no such thing. He kept silent all night long. In the morning the lion spotted a deer nearby and chased after it, finally giving up on the hunter and the bear.

"Please forgive me for my selfishness," the hunter told the bear as soon as the lion had left. "I am ashamed of myself. You protected me at the cost of your own safety and yet I betrayed your trust! I feel remorseful and guilty. Please have mercy on me!"

"I forgive you," the bear calmly replied. "Do not be afraid of any punishment." The bears' words disssolved the hunter's fears but he continued to feel very guilty. "Please help me get rid of my guilt," the hunter said, "or I won't be able to forgive myself all my life!" The bear reassured the hunter and gave him two pieces of advice.

"One," he said, "if you ever find yourself in a situation where someone has betrayed your trust, remember this incident and tell yourself, 'Even if I have been betrayed, I shall continue to have faith. Faith is what I stand for, come what may. That is how people shall know me.'"

"Second," he continued, "if the person, who has betrayed you, feels remorseful, tell him your story and ask that person to keep faith too. Treachery and betrayal are a disease that has gripped society today. People are not able to trust one another. By telling people your story, you will help people trust one another again and restore their faith."

The hunter thanked the bear for his help and his words of wisdom, climbed down the tree and went home. He was a transformed man, having learned the most important lesson of his life and being freed from guilt and remorse.

This fable illustrates how infallible faith in Nature keeps one safe in every situation. It was his pure faith that saved the bear from falling down to his death. It is said that one who has faith in God, has nothing to fear because once we place our faith in Nature, the all-knowing and infinitely wise Nature knows exactly how to save and guide us in every situation.

This fable is not just about a lesson one man learned. It has a deep and profound message for the entire mankind. The story is about how one can overcome betrayal of trust; about having faith, no matter what the situation is.

The fifth principle of faith states: **Betrayal is a myth. Faith is the truth.** Why is that? How can betrayal be a myth, and yet be a disease that has gripped mankind today?

Betrayal of faith is a myth because faith cannot be betrayed at all – provided the faith itself is unshakeable in the first place. A faith that gets betrayed, wasn't much of a faith to begin with. We hear people say, "I trusted him and yet he has betrayed me!" Quite often, we find ourselves in such situations where we say these words. Whenever we place our trust in someone and they behave in a way that is not in accordance with our interests or expectations, we feel betrayed.

In such times, it helps to remember that the other persons' actions were based on their faith. You do not have to cause your own faith to diminish due to their actions. Faith is the most powerful vibration of the universe and nothing can cause it to be destroyed. Hence, it can be said that betrayal of trust is a myth. Just the way darkness has no existence of its own; darkness is just the absence of light; betrayal of faith is simply the absence of faith.

In its adolescence, faith is invested in a particular person or situation. However, as faith grows, one learns that in addition to trusting individuals, it is important to also place one's faith in Nature.

When one receives anything, one assumes the channel through which he receives to be the source. As a result, he expects to receive further from the same channel and becomes disheartened if the channel does not deliver the goods.

For example, if one's brother, who used to help him earlier, stops helping him, he says, "My brother has let me down; he has betrayed me." If his father does not assign a fair share of his property to the son, then the son starts hating his father; he feels let down. This is so because people assume their relatives to be the givers, they place their faith on them.

We ignorantly invite situations of betrayal and sorrow when we expect from the channels around us. When we need water, we draw it from the tap. Does the tap have any capacity of giving? The tap is merely a channel for the water reservoir. There are many taps (channels) through which water is received, but they all come from the same water reservoir in the building. When we insist that we want water only from a particular tap, we are likely to invite sorrow in our lives.

If you seek water directly from the reservoir, you will get more than you could ever ask for. You give up your limited perspective of expecting from a particular channel. As a result, you realize that there are many other channels through which the source can possibly give. Everything is in abundance in the source. It is common sense to expect from the source, rather than the channels. When you place your faith in an individual person or situation, do not expect it in return from the same channel, expect it from the ultimate source, from the universe!

Does that mean we should never trust anybody? No! That's not what it means; the missing link here is that it is wrong to trust *only* individuals. There is a higher and subtler power that pervades everything and everyone; it is wiser to trust that, while we also trust its individual manifestations.

Consider the case of the bear. The bear decided to trust the hunter, but the hunter did not reciprocate. Eventually Nature took care of the bear. Even after the incident, the bear did not hold a grudge over the hunter because he trusted Nature; his actions were inspired by this faith. The bear found it in his heart to forgive the hunter and leave him with a lesson which helped propagate his faith further to even more people. That is an inspired act!

Hence, in situations where we feel that our faith is being questioned, we should remind ourselves that "I place my trust in Nature; in God; I trust the laws of Nature." When every action of ours is inspired by this faith, our faith matures.

Contemplate over the following questions to help your faith grow:

- How strong is my faith today compared to yesterday and how stronger can it be?
- What are the kinds of situations or incidents that touch my faith negatively?
- How can I make my faith steadfast even in such situations?
- How can I take my faith to such a height that it may never diminish at all?

These questions will help us know ourselves better and bring the current state of our faith to light. Once we know the current state, we can take steps towards making it stronger and better.

Faith-feedback System

We are understanding the importance of sowing and growing faith. We can always ask ourselves introspective questions to determine the state of our faith as listed above. However, wouldn't it be great to have a direct feedback mechanism? A Faith-feedback mechanism, so to say?

It is interesting to know that we already have such a mechanism in place!

Every situation in life, every incident we come across, is a mirror that reflects our faith.

In other words, anything that happens in your life is a feedback on your faith. The kind of response we give to situations and people shows us how deep or shallow our faith is and whether or not our actions are inspired by faith, or by the illusory reality that weighs down upon us. Whether we really have infallible faith deep within us, or it is just shallow words – situations bring out the truth.

> Two friends stayed in a village. One of them was skilled at rope-walking. He would earn money by doing roadshows. After every

few days, he would increase the height of the poles on which the rope was tied to further enhance his skills and make the show more entertaining. Every time he did that, he would ask his trusted friend, "Do you think I can do this?"

Each time his friend would reply, "Yes, I am confident you can do it!" He would then attempt it and succeed. A few weeks later, he decided to take his challenge to the next level. He decided to walk on a rope between two tall buildings. He asked his friend the same question, and he got the same answer, "Yes, I am confident you can do it!" He attempted the walk and was able to complete it successfully. This remarkable feat was published in the newspapers.

One day, he decided to walk on a rope tied between two hilltops! He asked his friend the same question and received the same answer. He attempted the walk and was successful. Finally, he decided to take on the ultimate challenge. He decided to walk the rope between the two hilltops carrying a person on his shoulders.

"Do you think this is possible?", he asked his friend.

"Absolutely!" his friend said, "you can surely achieve it!".

"Excellent then," he replied, "meet me tomorrow early morning at the foot of the hill."

"Why?" his friend asked.

"Who else can I carry on my shoulder but you, my old friend!" he replied, "No one else trusts me as much as you do!"

His friend seemed shaken up by this new turn! He began to tremble! His trust vanished in thin air! He was nowhere to be seen the next morning!

This incident served as a feedback for the friend. He got conclusive evidence that his faith was shallow. His assurance that his friend could achieve the feat were just mere words. As soon as he was placed in a situation where his faith was to be directly tested, he immediately backed out, because his trust was shaky, or rather nonexistent. His reaction to the situation clearly shows what his level of faith was.

Just like the friend, we see people around us say that they trust a certain person, but somewhere within, there is a fear of betrayal, some negativity harbored that manifests in the form of undesirable incidents in the person's life.

Betrayal is not an external event. It only reflects our own lack of infallible faith.

An electric bulb lights up only when the circuit is complete. Even a small disconnect leads to a broken circuit and the bulb wouldn't light up. Similarly, faith is the wire that connects us to Nature. If the circuit is complete, we see miracles. Even a small disconnect leads to a broken circuit and we never get to realize what we aspire for. We then blame the world, or Nature itself, for events that go against what we desire.

We should be able to perceive an undesirable situation as a mirror. The reaction we give to such a situation should help us see the state of our faith and immediately re-evaluate our actions. We need to allow faith to sponsor our actions. Only then can this circuit be complete and we see great results.

Nature is the mother of all and no mother wants to starve her children or deprive them of any resource. Wealth, health, happiness, peace, success – Nature is ever-obliging and *wants* to give us all of it. What then seems to be the hurdle? Our own inability to have faith in Nature; the inability to trust things that are yet unseen.

Whenever it feels like things are not happening for you, take a pause; use the situations around you as a feedback to check your faith.

Is my faith really as strong as I imagine?

Is there some subtle fear or doubt hidden within me?

Are there any specific people or situations that negatively affect my faith?

How can I make my faith immune to such people or situations?

> A woman who had just read in the Bible that faith can move mountains, was surprised by the statement and wondered if it were really true. She decided to put it to test.
>
> There was a hillock just behind her home. While going to bed, she looked at the hillock and said, "I have complete faith in God that tomorrow morning when I wake up, He would have moved this hill!"
>
> The next morning, she was disappointed to see that the hill hadn't budged even an inch. "I knew it!" she said, "It's impossible to move mountains!"

What kind of faith did the woman express in God? When she saw that her wish hadn't manifested the next day, she says she knew it won't. This shows that the faith she had expressed was shallow in the first place. She just wanted to test it. Her faith did not carry the conviction that "It is possible!"

Any doubt or distrust in faith will lead to a broken connection; which will manifest in the form of an undesirable situation or experience. Hence, instead of being disheartened by such incidents, use them as feedback to raise your faith and rectify your actions based on your faith. Only then shall the incident become a launchpad that propels you towards your goal.

The mind would want to sulk at every negative incident, thinking, "I am the victim here; why should I be the one to change my faith or do anything at all? What assurance do I have that I'll get whatever I want if I work on my faith? What proofs do I have?" Every person comes across these thoughts at some point in life. It is imperative to remember that in such times, we have to have faith in the unseen. We have to trust God; we have to trust Nature. It is important for completing the broken circuit that will lead to a glowing bulb. Sulking about the situation will not achieve this!

Consider a sick person, who visits a doctor to get treated. The doctor examines him and prescribes an injection, after which he will be completely cured. The person is afraid of injections and requests the doctor to cure him without it. The doctor explains that he has to gather the courage to endure the pain of an injection. It may be difficult, but it will lead him to faster recovery.

Similarly, when we want things to happen, Nature wants us to first take the pains to transform our faith. Thereafter, whatever we want is bound to come to us. However, most people stay in their comfort-zone and resist transformation. They continue to expect their desires to manifest *before* placing their faith. This is like the person who expects to be cured without the injection!

If a person is not able to achieve his goals in spite of all the hard work, he should not harbor negative feelings like, *"What's the use of working hard when my luck is rotten!"* Instead, he should analyze the entire episode and find where his faith was lacking. He needs to find out the loose connection in the circuit and realign his faith and actions.

We have to develop the perseverance of the farmer who, irrespective of how good or bad the rainfall has been during the previous year, continues to sows seeds every year, hoping for a good monsoon.

10

PRINCIPLE 6
TRANSFORMATION WITH 100 % FAITH

It is habitual for many people to complain that their life does not take shape as they wish. They feel that life is unfair and place the blame on various external factors.

We have seen how this is just the result of the beliefs that we harbor. Incidents in the external world reflect the beliefs we hold in our inner world.

What often troubles us is that despite placing our faith on a desired outcome, we do not see the desired change happening in our life. We forget that if the foundation is wrong, the building does not last long. We mistake our limiting beliefs to be our true faith. Contrary to this, our beliefs are shaded by the perceptions that we borrow from people around us and our experiences through life.

True faith develops when we trust ourselves in all situations, independent of any other influence. In the initial stages of this journey, faith does get boosted by favourable outcomes. However, unshakable faith is of a kind that is oblivious to external outcomes. This is faith in Nature, faith in God. It is the strongest form of faith where we are not attached to or dependent on any outcome. There is complete conviction that whatever Nature offers us is for our best. This is 100% faith.

100% faith is steadfast. It reflects a transition from the faith due to outside factors to faith in ourselves. When the game plan of life becomes clear to us, there is an automatic transformation to 100% faith. Just as water starts boiling and turns into steam only after it has reached 100 degree Celsius, internal transformation happens only when 100% faith is attained.

The sixth principle states that: **Inner transformation is brought about with 100% faith.**

100% faith might sound unreal, but there are examples in the real world which depict it. One such example is cited in the Bible. It describes a miracle that Jesus had worked. A disabled man, who had not been able to get up and stand since years, had heard of Jesus' miracles and strongly believed that He could help him. He had clarity and faith that Jesus would cure his ailment. According to the Bible, when Jesus came to meet this man and asked him to stand up, the man was able to do so with ease. This was possible because of his 100% faith in Jesus. There wasn't an iota of doubt in the man's mind and he had reached the stage of transformation where his faith was resolute.

This incident might seem to be miraculous, but it was possible due to the power of unflinching faith. The disabled man's foundation was strong; it was made of true 100% faith instead of the beliefs which are dependent on outside factors.

The steps leading to 100% faith are riddled with obstacles. This is because our faith is still in a developing stage. It is still partially dependent on others' opinions and our daily experiences. As we move up the stairs of faith, we tackle these obstacles and try to overcome them.

The first step in overcoming these hindrances is to contemplate them, so that they can be brought to light. Once we realize their futility, they begin to vanish. There are five such major types of obstacles in attaining 100% faith.

1. **Doubt and Distrust**

   It is common to have doubts and distrust. They are often mistaken to be self-defence mechanisms. We feel that we can be more secure and safe when we doubt the world. But, it's not doubting that is actually useful. It is the habit of questioning things without assuming them at face value that is useful.

   Doubting something leads to the clouding of the intellect. But, it gradually becomes a habit and the distrust that arises from it can shake the foundation of our faith. Distrust weakens our faith, which then begins to reflect in various facets of our life.

   Many people live in the illusion that doubting is necessary for life to be secure. They use it as a way to test loyalty in relations. This magnifies their sense of insecurity, which in turn begets even more occasions for doubts and distrust. It can also lead to losses and erode their faith.

   Instead of doubting faith, we should start questioning our own doubts. By doing this, we can rise above doubts and take a step toward 100% faith and transformation.

2. **Fear and Worry**

   Fear is another emotion that eventually causes us to worry. Fears can constrain us when they turn into a habit. Due to our fears, we try to escape from situations. This does not allow our faith to grow, thereby restricting our growth.

   Fear and worry eventually paralyze a person and restrain them from moving forward. To overcome fear and worry, we can take help of faith. Whenever fear grips us, we need to encourage ourselves by saying, "I can follow my faith despite the fear. I have faith in my faith and so I have nothing to fear. I have the capability to overcome every obstacle with peace and joy."

3. **Laziness**

   Procrastination is one of the major hurdles on our path to success. We tend to waste valuable time postponing tasks for later. This reduces our confidence. Laziness can dim our passion making us believe that we are just not set out for the task. All we need to do is overcome our laziness.

   We can start by setting small daily achievable targets and ensuring that we complete them the same day. We can try completing a task, part by part every day instead of doing it in a hurry, under pressure on the last day. This will help us regain our confidence. With every tick on the checklist, our faith will rise.

4. **Temptation**

   Temptation is a quicksand in which many have lost their footing. It drags us into distractions and derails us from achieving our goals.

   Temptation comes in many forms. It may be watching TV excessively or indulging in social media or browsing the internet indiscriminately. For a person on a diet, it may be their favorite food. It may even be in forms harmful to health such as alcohol or smoking. Such temptations distract us from achieving our goals. When we keep succumbing to our temptations over and over again, we end up losing our confidence. We start believing that it isn't possible for us to achieve a certain decided goal. This wrong belief, in turn, makes us underperform.

   Freeing ourselves from this quicksand requires patience and dedication. Whenever we are caught in the clutches of temptation, we must remind ourselves of our goal. Starting small, we can try to delay gratification. Every time we feel tempted to indulge in distractions, we can try to stretch ourselves a bit. The key is to remember that small gratifications now can lead to big disasters later, while a little more work done now can lead to satisfaction in the longer term. Gradually, we can overcome temptation to raise our faith.

5. **Fixations**

   The foundation of our belief system is set during our formative years. We believe whatever we hear or see around us. This mechanism may be helpful when a child is not capable of taking decisions. But once the child grows up, some of these beliefs become 'manufactured truths' or fixations, sponsored by parents, surroundings and the media. We don't challenge these fixations because it never occurs to us that something outside this frame of thinking is actually possible.

   Some examples of such fixations include

   - *"Women are not capable of doing certain tasks"* - This is a very common fixation which is deeply ingrained in our thinking. Many women lose faith and feel incapable due to this fixation

   - *"Women are sensitive, while men are rigid and emotionally strong"* - Many men try to hide their emotions and even feel ashamed of their emotions, as they are forced to conform with this belief.

   - *"Men are not supposed to cry"* - This is yet another common fixation. Men feel weak and stressed out in the effort to maintain a facade of strength. Such fixations can even affect their mental health and reduce their faith in themselves.

Despite such fixations, there are many inspiring examples of how overcoming social norms and having steadfast faith can lead to success. Dr Anandibai Joshi overcame all odds of gender discrimination to become the first lady from India to complete her MBBS in the early 1900s. Sudha Chandran broke every myth and fixation to do with her disability when she danced to the beat of music, despite having a prosthetic leg. Dhirubhai Ambani worked hard day and night, and rose from humble beginnings to founding Reliance Industries.

All of these people have demonstrated that anything is possible, be it playing a sport or performing an art after an accident or founding an entire business house despite their humble background. All these examples show how faith in oneself can lead one to the heights of success, even in the material world. When our faith reaches 100%, we experience a transformation of beliefs within us. Inner transformation leads to success in our worldly activities as well.

Raising our faith requires consistency, dedication and most importantly, faith on oneself.

> A wave from the ocean was feeling very unimportant and minuscule. It didn't have faith that it could be worthy of anything as it found itself negligable in comparison to the ocean. It is only when the wave was made to contemplate its true nature that it realized its oneness with the ocean. The wave was the ocean itself in essence; it was the expression of the ocean. Such is the kind of realization that catapults faith to 100%.

Just like the wave, we humans are none other than the Source in our essence. We see ourselves as being individial and separate from Nature, which limits our faith in our potential and constrains our life. Once we begin to realize our oneness with the Source, we open up to our highest possibilities. When we develop 100% faith, our lives can be transformed into something new and much more powerful.

Raising faith is a continuous process. The daily practice of Faith meditation can help in this process.

Following are the steps to practice Faith meditation. You can record the affirmations given below and play them when you are seated in a comfortable posture with eyes closed. It helps to speak out the affirmation along with the recording.

1. Close your eyes and be seated in a comfortable posture.
2. Tell yourself, "I am practicing Faith meditation. This will help me elevate my faith and release any doubts and distrust from within me."
3. Take a few deep breaths and relax.
4. Repeat the following affirmations with faith.
    a. I am infinite. I am one with Nature.
    b. I am pure. I am filled with love, joy, and peace.
    c. I can always be happy. I can lead a life filled with happiness.
    d. I am complete. I am enough. Being complete, I am happily completing every task on time.
    e. Every experience is helping me grow and learn. I am capable of achieving more and more day by day.
    f. I have let go of my ego and am open to the free flow of Nature.
    g. I am healthy and fit. All the parts of my body are functioning like a song.
    h. All my relations are based on the foundations of love, peace, and joy. All my relations are pure and filled with harmony and good intentions.
    i. I am fearless and brave. I have infinite strength, love, joy, time, money, self-confidence.
    j. I am free, I am freedom. I am open and receptive to the ways of Nature.
    k. Everything that happens in my life is smoothly leading me towards my ultimate purpose.

5. Remain immersed in the feeling of faith and deep assurance that these affirmations stir within you.

6. Slowly open your eyes,

These affirmations will help strengthen our faith and take us further on the path towards 100% faith, leading to inner transformation. Being aware of our increasing faith and the positive effect it has on our life, we can help others raise their faith too.

11

PRINCIPLE 7
THE ULTIMATE EVOLVED STATE OF FAITH

A bird that has been caged for a long time keeps looking up at the sky when its cage is opened. It feels paralyzed and debilitated to be able to leave the cage. Despite being pushed and prodded, it stays inside and is reluctant to fly out.

Why? Because the bird assumes the walls of the cage to be the limits of its world. For the bird, the limits of the cage seem so real! It lacks faith that it can fly out of its confines. It has accepted the cage to be its farthest boundaries; its limitation. Its brain is incapable of thinking of a life outside the cage because it has assumed its limitation to be the ultimate truth.

So is the case with human life. The faith that lies buried within us gets encumbered by the limits imposed in our own thoughts. We dream of reaching the heights of success, but our own disbelief stops us from getting there. Like the limits of the cage that seem real to the bird, the limits that are apparent in our thoughts seem very real to us. Like the bird in the cage, we accept our limitations and often end up doing nothing more than staring at the sky, that we dream of flying in.

Our deep longing is to expand and be like the sky. And that's because openness and grandeur are our true nature. Until we realize our fullest potential, we always feel a void within, that calls out at us constantly. We feel hampered and suffocated by limitations, but we also easily get used to them and stay in their comfort zone.

Most people dream to soar high, but live as victims of circumstances, not realizing that they are actually victims of their own thoughts that cage them. On the contrary, if they have faith in the providence of the universe, they can muster courage to take flight and soar high.

Nature is driving everything and everyone – without exception - towards evolution. You will see that everything from people to countries, machines to technologies – everything is evolving. Nothing remains stagnant. Everything changes, everything grows. This is applicable to our faith as well. Our faith too, evolves.

The seventh principle of faith states: **Everything in Nature is automatically and effortlessly progressing towards its state of ultimate evolution. When faith evolves into its utmost state, it becomes Divine Faith.**

When we have conviction on the efficacy of this principle, we offer the Universe the opportunity to operate our lives in auto-pilot mode, being open to the unfolding of our highest possibilities.

The Cycle of Progressive Evolution

When we encounter problems in life, we may feel intimidated or take it as a challenge. A problem appears to be a problem when it is viewed through the lens of limiting beliefs. If we look at the so-called problems of our life with the eye of faith, they are opportunities for progress, the harbingers of growth and evolution.

Progressive evolution is cyclical in nature. Every so-called problem or challenge occurs in our life so that we develop our capability and unleash our potential. It prods us to develop qualities within us and manifests the next state of evolution in life. When we learn, grow and make progress, we attain succeess in overcoming the challenge. Every success, in turn, brings with it the next level of challenges. So the cycle of evolution keeps going this way: Challenge >>> Progress >>> Success >>> Next challenge.

Divine Evolution

We are all well acquainted with the word evolution and regression. Evolution means growth, development. People make plans for their development, most of them stick to their plans and are even successful in life. This is the evolution in the materialistic world and the happiness derived therein. Regression is the opposite; the falling back to a lower state.

However, when we speak of *Divine evolution*, we are referring to the development or growth that is beyond the dualities of evolution and regression. It is a state where a person's evolution has attained a state where his happiness is not subject to his external conditions.

The word 'Divine' adds a special meaning; a whole new perspective to whichever word it is prefixed with. For example *Divine love* is an evolved state of love that transcends the dualities of love and hate. A person who has evolved to a state where he experiences Divine love for everyone and everything, has gone beyond the dualities of love and hate. Love, although a positive feeling in itself, brings attachment, which is the cause for sorrow and other negative emotions. So a person who has Divine love has not only conquered the outright negative emotions of hate, but also conquered the subtler aspect of attachment that comes with love. He has achieved a state that is beyond the two dualities.

Similarly, *Divine joy* is the happiness that lies beyond the dualities of happiness and sorrow. One is neither affected by sorrow nor attached to happiness.

Likewise, Divine evolution is the ultimate state of evolution, wherein the person has evolved beyond the possibility of regressing back. He is beyond that duality because he is freed of his ego, fears, greed, hatred, desires and all such vulnerabilities. When a person gains wealth, fame, position, and honor, he is said to have materially grown or evolved. This evolution takes place on the basis of his faith. This journey of material growth, in turn, even strengthens his faith. However, when one begins the inward journey towards Self-realization, one moves towards *Divine evolution*. With this inward journey, one's faith transcends to the state of *Divine faith*.

What is Divine faith?

Simply said, Divine Faith is when one begins to have faith in faith itself. One realizes that it is faith that drives life; one realizes that only Divine faith can lead one to realizing their fullest potential. Before this state, it is all about whether you have faith or you don't. After this point, there is no duality. There only remains faith and the faith in faith. There remains absolutely no scope for disbelief, doubts, hesitation or distrust.

Every step in the journey of evolution of faith is designed to culminate at this pinnacle. Setbacks, challenges, difficult relationships, testing circumstances – all of these are designed to awaken this ultimate evolved state.

We all know the story of Prince Siddhartha, who despite being the son of a king and the heir to a prosperous kingdom, renounced his worldly possessions and ambitions in pursuit of the true Self. He was sensitive to sorrow and was overwhelmed by the suffering he observed around him. Sorrow played a pivotal role in directing him towards his divine purpose. He dedicated himself to severe penance and experimented with various modalities of meditation towards attaining liberation. This journey transformed Prince Siddhartha into the Buddha. He attained the ultimate state of evolution – Divine evolution.

With Self-realization, one experiences the answer to the question, "Who am I?" This is a question that has no answer that can be explained in words. It can only be experienced.

Imagine that you are at a party and you smell a very sweet perfume that someone at the party has applied. You love the smell but later on, when you are trying to describe it to someone, how do you do it?! How can you describe the fragrance? The only words that you might use are beautiful, sweet, mesmerizing. But these are all common words – they still only go as far as to say something is nice. But the experience itself cannot be put in words!

Likewise, the answer of the question "Who am I?" is the experience of the true Self. It is indescribable. When one experiences the bliss of the true Self and gets established in that experience, it is the state of Divine evolution.

Through centuries, there have been many great saints and prophets on earth who have attained this state of Self-realization – Jesus, Prophet Muhammad, Guru Nanak, Saint Meera, Saint Dnyaneshwar and so on. Many of these saints, in turn, inspired and guided others on their spiritual journey to attain the same state.

It remains for us to embark on this journey ourselves, towards our own Divine evolution that will transform our faith to its ultimate evolved state – Divine faith.

Beyond logic and preconditions

Based on where faith is placed, it can be categorized as:

- Faith on one's own senses
- Faith on a trustworthy person
- Divine Faith

Let us look at each one and see how our own faith is subject to this categorization.

Faith on one's own senses

This is the kind of faith that we have only on the experiences that come from our own senses. We experience a deep attachment with our body – our physical form and the sensory organs that come with it. Any experience that comes within the purview of our senses is like a first-hand experience for us; hence it becomes very easy for us to believe and accept it as the final truth.

Even if a close and trustworthy person were to tell us that something that we have experienced through our senses is wrong or an illusion, we would choose to believe our senses rather than the person. This is because the experience that comes through the senses feels most logical and rational. It is easy to believe because of our sheer proximity to the source of the experience.

> Samir was taking a walk one evening when he saw his close friend, Jay, walk past him. As he walked past him, Samir saw Jay make a face and say, "You are such a fool!" Samir was furious about Jay's behavior and upset that he did not even stop to speak to him properly. He did not speak to Jay for several days.
>
> Jay noticed this and one day he approached Samir and asked him why he was keeping aloof. Samir told him he was upset because of Jay's rude behavior the other day. Jay laughed, "But I wasn't talking to you! I had my earphones on and I was talking to my colleague when I said that!" However, in spite of this explanation, Samir found it difficult to believe Jay, because he had heard him say the words and seen him make a face at him.

This is an example of how we often tend to have more faith in our own senses than anything or anybody else.

Is it wrong to trust our senses then? Are they always wrong?

No! It is not being said that it is wrong to trust our senses. However, it is wrong to *always* trust only our senses. It is important to acknowledge that the truth can be beyond what the senses experience; like in the case of Samir and Jay. It is wrong to say that only that which we see, hear, touch, smell or taste is rational and is hence the truth.

Faith on a trustworthy person

The second kind of faith is the faith we place in the trustworthy people in our lives. This faith too, to an extent is largely based on logic and rationale and to some extent on emotions. This kind of faith makes us trust the people whom we consider trustworthy, even if what they say does not confirm to the experiences of our senses.

In some cases, we may not have a sensory experience of something at all; so we trust these people and take their word as truth. This applies mostly to children, who have faith in what their parents and teachers say instead. They are easily able to believe what they are told.

Most people have someone in their life, in whom they have complete faith and whose words they blindly accept. Such faith, of course, does not develop overnight. If there is some such person in our lives, and we ask ourself how we came to trust that person so much, we will realize that there is always some reason or rationale behind it. For example, a person has faith in a friend, because he has found that the friend's suggestions have always benefitted him. So this becomes the rationale behind the person's faith in his friend. However, if at some point in life, some suggestion of the friend were to cause him any harm, he could lose his faith.

So you will see that such faith is also based on a condition that is fulfilled. It cannot be called unconditional or unshakeable. It cannot be permanent, because the external world is subject to change. Any faith that is affected by changing logic or conditions is not faith, but just a shadow of it.

Divine Faith

Divine faith is the final and the ultimate evolved state of faith. The first two kinds of faith are not completely futile. They can be considered as phases of faith as it evolves; milestones on the journey to Divine faith. These two kinds of faiths do help us reach the final goal.

Divine faith is the unconditional faith that has gone beyond dualities. It is not based on any logic, any rationale or any condition that *has to be* satisfied for the faith to continue.

But why do we need divine faith at all? What is the need to have such ultimate and unquestioning faith in something or someone? Isn't it true that the world can function even with less or probably no Divine faith at all?

It is not true that people who do not have Divine faith will never be successful. They will be, but there is a limit to that success. This success is limited to the material world. When it comes to the spiritual plane – the journey inwards – one needs to have Divine faith. Those who wish to go beyond their worldly existence, understand the Final Truth of life, and bring about their Divine evolution, have to transform their faith into Divine faith.

With the awakening of Divine faith, life becomes aligned with the divine purpose of all creation. There remains no individual personalized agenda for life; one leads an impersonal life, serving the larger purpose of the Universal 'I'. The false 'I' – the ego – is transcended and one operates from the bliss of Self-realization.

Hence, let us persevere for Divine evolution; to understand and apply the principles of faith, so that our faith evolves into Divine faith, so that we may attain the utmost evolved state of being in this very life. Let this prayer be offered not just for ourselves, but for all living beings.

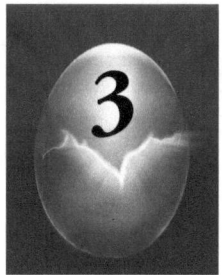

BEYOND FAITH

When one reaches the culmination of the journey in the evolution of faith, one transcends it. Life operates from the limitless standpoint. This part of the book discusses the flowering of life beyond Divine faith.

12
TRANSCENDENCE OF FAITH

The way laws work in the unseen realm go beyond logic. The fixed logic that we use in the material world does not apply in the spiritual realm. What is believed to work in the material world is in stark contrast to the way life actually works in the unseen.

In the material world, it is logical to believe that: *When you give, you lose; when you receive, you gain.* However, in the unseen realm: **When you give, you gain; when you lose, you find.**

People chase after acquiring wealth and possessions based on the belief that: *The more you accumulate, the happier you will be.* But the truth of how it actually works in the unseen is: **The more you let go, the happier you are.**

In the context of faith, this is even more relevant. Most people may believe that: *You've got to see it to believe it.* But the way it works in the unseen is: **Believe it with unshakeable conviction and you shall get to see it.**

And when one transcends faith, when on goes beyond beliefs, the way it works in the unseen is: **When you can See, then there is no need to believe.** Seeing, in this context, implies knowing. When one directly knows the unseen through direct experience, then there is no question of placing faith or having belief.

For us, who has grown up in the material world, who have believed in the firm logic of the material world, the illogical ways of the unseen are naturally hard to accept. In such a realm where logic does not apply, the faith that has to be expressed has to transcend all logic and rationale. It is only by having Divine faith in the Universe or God that one can complete one's spiritual journey and attain the ultimate state of being, which is our true essence.

Some people *think* they believe in God. "I have complete faith in God," they say, but as soon as something untoward happens, their faith is shaken up. "How could God do this to me!" Their faith is only an illusion, a shadow of true faith.

What would one, who has Divine faith in God, say?

"By not granting my wish, God is preparing me with a precious lesson for my own betterment. Let me try and learn it. I am sure my wish will eventually manifest. My gratitude to God for His grace!"

Ask yourself contemplative questions on your faith: "Does my faith in God depend on some logic or pre-condition? If yes, what is it? Can I say that my faith in God will remain steadfast even when such rationale or pre-conditions are not satisfied?"

Upon contemplation, we will find that rationale and conditions will change with time, place and person, because everything in the world – except Divine faith – is subject to change. This is the reason why Divine faith has such an important role to play in life. The lessons of life that unfold on the path to realizing the Final Truth, are often illogical. Hence, only one who has Divine faith can imbibe such lessons.

For example, when it is said that, "Life is effortless and happening in autopilot," a novice to this concept may find it hard to accept it. "How can life be so easy?" he may think. But when he decides to keep faith and apply this truth in daily life, he discovers its truth through his own experience. "Believe with unshakeable conviction, and you shall get to see it!" He gets a first-hand experience of the ease of life; this becomes the basis for his faith and his faith begins to grow.

The ultimate faith is attained when it grows beyond all reason and logic. So, you see that his faith begins with logic but eventually reaches a state where it transcended it. Let us understand the Guru-disciple relationship with the help of a story:

> A person once came to the Buddha's hermitage and requested his disciples to allow him to meet the Buddha. Once he was in His company, he asked Him, "I have a lot of questions and doubts about God and His ways. I have wandered everyplace looking for answers, but in vain. Please answer my questions and I shall be eternally grateful to You!"
>
> Buddha calmly listened to his plea and when he was done, spoke, "All your questions shall be answered and all your doubts quelled. However, there is a condition. You must give me a year of your life. You must stay here for a year, be a part of the hermitage and engage yourself in selfless service, without asking a single question or expecting any answer."
>
> The person was surprised by this condition but decided to comply as he was desperate for answers. He had wandered seeking answers and decided to keep faith on Buddha and give it one last chance. He began his life at the hermitage, learned the way of life there, began to take part in the daily schedule of cleaning, cooking food, prayer and other chores. He would spend time everyday reading, contemplating and meditating.
>
> The year raced by and he realized that his questions and doubts about God had dissolved. His faith in the Buddha's way of teaching was strengthened. His last attempt did not go in vain. By persistently listening to his Guru's words, and by studying and meditating upon them, he had received the answers to all his questions – even the ones that hadn't occurred to him!
>
> By having faith in his Guru and imbibing all the illogical lessons he taught, the disciple had received the ultimate benefit.

One may not have Divine faith in the Guru – the one who shows the way in life – from the very beginning. In fact, the initial faith is very rational. However, once we place faith in a true Guru, there comes a point in the journey when we stop expecting truths to conform to our logic, before we believe them. At this stage, our faith on the Guru helps us trust every word he says, without the need for any evidence.

To attain the ultimate evolved state of being, we need to bring flexibility in our thinking. We have to question our assumptions, doubts and beliefs. We need to rise above logic and rationale because the Final Truth transcends the limits of the human intellect. Most people only believe what they see, but those who are able to place faith in the unseen are the ones who experience miracles. Divine faith is the apex of faith. Attaining Divine faith is the ultimate purpose of life.

> Sage Narada – the reverred devotee-disciple of Lord Vishnu – was once wandering around the Himalayan foothills, singing hymns. He came across two young men sitting a short distance apart under two trees, eyes closed in a meditative posture.
>
> Hearing the sage's hymns, the two young men opened their eyes to see who it was. Beholding Sage Narada, they hurriedly got up and touched his feet. After blessing them, Sage Narada inquired what they were doing sitting under a tree in the forest. One of them spoke up, "Our salulations to you, Great Sage! We belong to the nearby village; we have spent the last couple of years practicing meditation here to attain *Moksha*."
>
> "Ah, that is good," said Narada, "please carry on. Am sorry to have disturbed you."
>
> The two young men looked at each other hesitantly, stopping themselves from speaking out. Sensing their hesitation, Narada asked them, "What is it that you wish to say? Go ahead and say it unhesitatingly."

"O Great Sage," replied one of them, "You are known to have great foresight and we wish to ask you a question."

"Go ahead" said Narada.

"Can you please tell us how long will it take for us to attain liberation?"

Narada smiled and closed his eyes for a few moments while the two young men waited in anticipation. When he opened his eyes, they both looked at him expectantly.

"You," he pointed to one of the young men, "shall attain Moksha in this very life." The young man that he was referring to was startled at this pronouncement. He got up hurriedly.

"Where are you going?" asked Narada. "I must hurry home," said the young man, "I have so many things to do before I attain Moksha. I have to travel the world, get married, have children, build a home for myself. I better get on with all those things." Saying thus, he left for the village.

"And me?" asked the second man, "When do I attain Moksha, dear Sage?"

"You, my dear man, will need to take as many births as there are leaves on this tree, before you attain Moksha."

Sage Narada expected the young man to be disappointed. Instead his face lit up and he was overwhelmed with joy! "That is wonderful," he said with a wide and satisfied smile, "at least now I have a number that God has set for me!"

The young man closed his eyes, folded his hands and started dancing in gratitude to God for blessing him with Moksha.

Just as this happened, a strong gust of wind came through and blew away all the leaves on the tree, leaving none behind!

A smile spread across Sage Narada's face as he realized what that meant. He chanted Lord Vishnu's name, blessed the young man who was lost in divine rapture, and walked away!

This story illustrates the divine faith that the young man had in God. Instead of feeling depressed that he had to go through so many lifetimes before attaining liberation, he found unquestioned joy in the certainty that he was to attain Moksha, even if it was after so many births. His reaction to the incident is a clear indication of his unflinching faith. As soon as he expressed this Divine faith, he was rewarded. There was no place for doubt in his mind and nothing was impossible for his faith.

Divine faith does not seek to be rewarded, and yet, it never goes unrewarded!

Pessimists, who do not believe in Moksha or believe that it is impossible to attain Moksha in this very birth, lead a life of bondage. Such bondage first develops in the mind and then begins to manifest in various facets of their lives.

On the other hand, one who has Divine faith, leads a life of Divine freedom – a state of liberation from both, freedom and bondage. When one is established in the state of Divine faith, on is liberated from the rise and fall of the ego, from the push and pull of the material world, from thoughts, emotions and past conditioning.

If we believe that liberation is only attainable after many births and after undergoing great hardships and efforts, that becomes our faith and that is how Nature complies. If we believe that Self-realization is the birthright of every human being and that it is attainable in this very lifetime while we are alive, then that's the possibility that we open ourselves to. Every spoken word is an expression of faith. Hence, it helps to contemplate on the words that we speak repeatedly to gauge the state of our faith. Are we moving toward Divine faith yet?

Of all the beings that were created, only humans have been gifted with the ability to think and make higher choices that align with the

Heart. However, most people use this ability to only gain material success, as we have forgotten the true purpose of human life. While it is not wrong to seek and attain material success, it does not give us true fulfilment to be satisfied and stop there.

Very few want to go beyond the material world to experience who-they-truly-are. Many people traverse through their entire life without giving this question so much as a fleeting thought. Only we humans have the possibility of attaining Self-realization and being established in that experience.

Divine Faith transcends the Faith Frame

With the awakening of Divine faith, one no longer needs an external reason to have faith. Faith is steadfast. It does not matter to one whether or not wishes are fulfilled, because such faith is not dependent on any action or its outcome.

At this ultimate stage of evolution, there is no question of keeping faith in something or placing faith in someone. This is because, life becomes an expression of faith itself. The individual ego, which believed it was "placing" faith in something or someone, surrenders to the flow of life.

We have discussed the first principle of faith where we saw the Faith Frame with the four corners of Faith, Feeling, Action and Result. We discussed how faith affects feelings, feelings inspire actions leading to the result; and how the result in turn reinforces the faith. We also discussed how, for most people, reinforcement of the faith is based only on results of their actions. This means that the strength of the faith is based on the results of actions. If the result tallies with what was desired, the faith grows stronger; if not, it diminishes. Faith, in the context of the Faith frame, is conditional.

With the transcendence of faith, one goes beyond the faith frame. The first three aspects continue, but the final step – the effect of results on faith – doesn't exist. If one gets the desired result, that's good. If one doesn't, that's still good, because of the conviction that the Divine flow must have a reason for not bringing about the particular outcome at this time. It doesn't mean God is saying, 'No'; it means God is saying 'Not now'.

There are limitless possibilties in the unseen that cannot be fathomed by the human intellect. Divine faith outgrows reason and becomes fully open to unseen possibilities. For the one, who is established in Divine faith, Faith is the starting point at all times. Results are a mere bonus.

One functions from the sheer joy of being oneself! Let us understand more about this in the next chapter – Starting from the finishing line.

13
STARTING FROM THE FINISHING LINE

If you tell a child, "Go and play outside for some time, and I will gift you a box of chocolates." What would the child say? He would be surprised – getting to play outside is a gift in itself. What more could he ask for!

The child doesn't need a gift or anything in return to play. Playing itself is a gift for him; his joy lies in playing. Why would he expect anything in return for it? Playing, in itself, is joy for the child!

But when it comes to the game of life, do we play it for the utter joy of it!? With every activity that we engage in, our interest lies in what we will get out of it. Most often, it is the fruit of action that motivates us, more than the action itself.

The best dancers immerse themselves into their art to the point where they do not identify themselves separately as performers of their art; they become one with the performance. When they are dancing on stage, we may see it as a person dancing flawlessly, but to them the only thing on stage is nature taking its course. There is no person. There is no ego.

If only we could live in such spontaneous flow of life; then we wouldn't be acting *for* happiness; rather we would be acting *from* joy! This is the hallmark of a life that has transcended faith.

If we gain the perspective of playing the game of life, then we will participate in every activity sportingly, with a playful attitude. And when we learn to participate in life this way, then the beneficial results or consequences of our actions would become mere bonuses. Our actions would be an expression of joy in themselves!

When you reach the state where you don't need any motivation from the external world, then what do you place your faith on? There's nothing left to place faith on! Your very presence then becomes faith-in-action.

Nothing will then seem difficult, for all the so-called difficulties will be challenges that we welcome. Challenges make the game more interesting to play. We would be truly living from the state of freedom if we didn't need any additional motivation for action.

That you are alive, in itself, is the whole and sole inspiration for action!

The Trouble with Acting from Expectations

While negative deeds bear negative consequences, virtuous deeds need not necessarily bear good consequences. Instead, they could bear a mixed bag of both happiness and sorrow. If you hold expectations of admiration or other gains in return for your actions or you consider yourself righteous because of your good deeds, then your streak of happiness is destined to hit the wall of sorrow eventually.

Sure, good deeds bring a fulfilling feeling of righteousness. But if you find yourself attached to such feelings, then any impedance in their flow can shake your faith. You cannot be possessive of something that is temporary in its very nature. If you are possessive about acquiring and preserving what you gain from your actions, then the smallest of slumps will take you down the spiral of sorrow. Therefore, good deeds are not the means to an end. We must aim beyond good deeds to selfless deeds that are devoid of expectations.

If you are not attached to the fruits of your actions then it makes them selfless. To give an example, when you bathe every day, you do not do it for want of admiration. In fact, you do not expect anything in return because the very act of cleansing yourself is a fruit in itself! Cleanliness is your very nature. When you live by your very nature, you do not expect anything in return.

So, when we do not expect praise in return for bathing, why must we expect it in return for cooking meals, or for earning a livelihood, or for doing well on a project at the workplace?

If you cook a meal with creativity, love and pure intention, then you have already reaped the fruits of your actions, regardless of the praise you may receive for it. However, if you feel disturbed or offended if not praised, you would not only be postponing your joy, but also making it conditional. Your joy would then be subject to the responses of others.

Immersing yourself in action

Whether you are cooking a meal in the kitchen, or working in the office, immerse yourself fully in it. There are many such examples that personify selflessness. Why do we remember Mother Teresa? Because she was immersed in selfless service. There was no desire for anything in return. If there was a desire, then work wouldn't even begin.

When a dancer is at the peak of the dance performance, the dancer is immersed in it, such that she ceases to be a separate entity. She has become one with the dance. All that remains is the dance. When this happens, the performance reaches the highest expression.

So it is with every activity that we engage in. When you immerse yourself in it, when you become one with it, the quality of the action is raised. There is no separate 'you' that would expect anything in return for the action. Then the action itself is the reward for you.

Sometimes we do find ourselves immersed in the moment for the joy of it – perhaps while listening to music or while dancing. We love going on vacations because it is easy for us to forget ourselves in the lap of nature. We need to bring similar feelings into all our actions.

Playing for the sake of playing

When you participate in a running race, you run to win. Your aim is to cross the finishing line before anyone else does. Your happiness does not lie in the starting position; you see it far away – beyond the finishing line. You hold expectations of winning the race and your faith can fluctuate when you're attached to the result.

But what if you were to start from the finishing line? You participate in the race because you have already won! You run because you are happy. The consequence of the race does not really matter to you, for you are already experiencing the joy of touching the finishing line at the very beginning. For you, running itself is joy. You play for the sake of playing, not winning.

What has happened here? Here, you are not acting to gain joy. You are already in joy, and action arises from joy!

If this is the case, then what are your expectations? There's nothing to expect! And since you are not attached to anything, there's no question of a fluctuating faith. Your faith remains steadfast as it is based on the changeless.

Shift your vibration to the feeling of 'Havingness'

One who believes that he is not enough or that he does not have enough, feels drained of energy and depressed all the time. This feeling becomes the undercurrent during his daily chores and activities.

How are you feeling right now? This question does not pertain to any ongoing situation or incident. It is directed at the deepest core of your being. How do you feel right now? The answer may not occur in words, but may perhaps emerge as a feeling of lack, or incompleteness, or unrest. This is the vibration that you are aligned with at the moment.

It is indeed possible to shift our core vibration to that of divine faith, abundance – the feeling of 'havingness'. We need to learn to shift our vibration by just choosing it. It is a conscious choice that we can make. Adopt the perspective of abundance, to be a "have" as against being a "have-not".

The past or the future are not your reality. The only reality for you is the present moment. Being in the present moment is complete in itself. The happiness that it can deliver has no dependencies or prerequisites. We can choose to be happy right here, right now.

Whatever we do – read, work, drive, cook, clean – savor the act and feel the joy in it. Close your eyes for a moment and ask yourself, "Is this moment full of joy and wonder?" Feel the moment before you answer that and you will find that the answer shifts you to the vibration of abundance, of havingness.

Most people unconsciously choose to align with the vibration of scarcity. They live as 'have-nots'. When this feeling of scarcity is at the root of their actions, the expression will obviously be negative, further reinforcing the feeling of being a have-not.

When you shift your vibration and align it with the perspective of abundance, you will notice that abundance, love, joy and peace begin to manifest effortlessly in a natural free flow. Let us further our understanding about this from the following example:

> Jim had been desperately looking for a job for a long time and had applied at many places. The primary thought in his mind though was that "I do not have a job! I am not receiving positive responses from anywhere!"
>
> Then one day, he received a call from one of the places. They informed him that he had been selected. He was overjoyed. He finally had a job!
>
> As it happened, in the following week, he received responses from the other places as well. They too informed him that he had cleared the interviews at those places as well!

How did this happen? What brought about these manifestations?

When Jim received the first positive reply, he was shifted from the vibration of scarcity to that of abundance, from a 'have-not' to a 'have'. This shift in vibration manifested this possibility in his life.

Consider the example of a woman who is not able to conceive. The predominant thought in her mind is "I am *not* able to conceive. I do *not* have a child." Then someone suggests her to adopt a child. She does that and the thought changes to "I *have* a child!" and shortly thereafter, she does conceive!

Such is the wonderful magic of the feeling of havingness. When we establish ourselves in this feeling, everything naturally begins to lead to the best possible outcome. All challenges seem to automatically find miraculous solutions.

We have been programmed to believe that we can gain happiness through whatever we do. And we continue believing this without doubt because we see everyone else around us in the same pursuit. This makes us seek happiness in the world.

The world can never bring us lasting joy. Doing something cannot bring us joy. Action is not the means to joy. True action flows *from* joy, from the feeling of 'havingness'. When we truly understand this profound truth, we will stop playing the game of life to win or acquire. We would have overcome the illusion of the pursuit for happiness. What follows is a state of detached enthusiasm.

Dispassionate passion – the Primal Creative Force

Who-you-truly-are is beyond the mind and body. You are pure awareness, which precedes thoughts and emotions. Everything that happens is within the light of awareness, but awareness remains ever-complete and ever-untouched by the happenings of the world. Thus, indifference or dispassion is the nature of awareness. It is your true nature.

When there is clarity of your indifferent nature, then you can participate in the activities of the world with a kind of *dispassionate* passion. You do not have any fixations for outcomes. Whatever you wish for, you may get it, or you may not get it. But you will continue to enthusiastically wish for it, although it doesn't really matter to you whether or not you get it!

With such detachment, you are not at loggerheads with whatever *is*. You love and allow whatever is to be as it is. There is no struggle or conflict. Such detachment can only arise from your unshakeable conviction in who-you-truly-are.

This can be called dispassionate passion.

Dispassionate passion is the primal creative force; it is original creative power of the universe! If it were not for this quality of dispassion, then there would be no creation. It is such detached interest that brings about the creation of the phenomenal world. If there is even an iota of attachment or fixation in the creative process, then what gets created is limited and not sustainable for long. Attachment to outcomes limits our creative potential. Attachment collapses possibilities from the unseen.

When we lead life with this attitude of indifference in whatever is, it brings forth the qualities of courage and freedom. Whether you are making a business deal or attending a job interview, if you are indifferent to the outcome of the deal or interview, then you experience a freedom of a different kind.

If you are attached to the outcome, then it causes a struggle in an attempt to force a particular outcome. Such struggle involves a forced effort, which can trigger disturbing feelings within. And as we have seen, feelings affect our actions and determine the results.

Whether you win the business deal or not, whether you get selected for the job or not, your faith does not falter when you are detached. Choices and actions that are apt for the given situation effortlessly emerge from this state of dispassionate passion.

14
THE STATE BEYOND FAITH

A discussion on the state beyond faith necessitates the discussion of the state before all creation.

What is the state of the Creator before creation?

The original state of the Creator or Self is at a state of rest when the world is not yet created – an unexpressed state in which the Self alone exists. This is the state in which the experiencer is present, but cannot experience Himself. (*Here, though we use the word "Himself", it is implied that the Self is beyond gender. The use of "him" or "her" is only a matter of convenience.*)

When there is only one without another, one cannot know oneself; one cannot realize one's own presence. It is only when there is another that one can feel one's presence. To experience its own presence, it can be said that the Self-at-rest brings about the state of the Self-in-action – the expression of the Self. The subject creates the object to experience its own presence. When the Self expresses itself as the subject (mind) and the object (the world), it is the state of the Self-in-action. The Self experiences itself through expression.

However, when the Self gets identified with the mind and body, it assumes, "I am the mind, I am these thoughts, I am this body." This gives rise to the illusion of there being many different bodies and many different selves, due to the imagined sense of separateness. If I am 'this' body, I assume that I am not 'that' body, or 'those' bodies.

Whatever is inside the body is assumed to be 'I', and whatever is outside appears to be 'others'. This is merely a projection, an illusion of separateness that the Self gets entangled in. In this entanglement and false identification, the real purpose of this grand expression – the purpose of experiencing the Self's presence – is forgotten.

When the Self begins to dis-entangle itself from this illusion of separateness, Self-witnessing gains precedence over interest in the world. The ultimate purpose is realized only when there is a permanent shift from witnessing the world to "witnessing the witnesser".

While looking into a mirror, the purpose of the mirror is not served if you do not see yourself. In the same way, while witnessing the world, the focus should shift to witnessing the Self; the focus should shift to knowing the knower. The world serves as a mirror to bring awareness of the knower's presence.

Self-realization is the realization of the true purpose of the Self in creating this world. The real 'I' is realized. With the experience of Self-realization, the knower of everything becomes self-aware.

However, a one-time glimpse does not serve the purpose, because the conditioning of the mind kicks in and pulls awareness back into the world. The real purpose is to be established permanently in the experience of the Self. This can be called Self-stabilization. When the Self stabilizes in Self-experience, there is no more risk of returning to the ego-centric conditioning. All conditioning is transcended.

When Self-stabilization is attained, one gets established in unshakeable conviction about the non-existence or falsehood of the separate individual is established. The original nature of the Self is recognized. The Self continues to act, but it does not identify with the mind and the body.

After Self-stabilization, when thoughts arise in the mind, there is no feeling that these are my thoughts. The understanding is that this thought has appeared because it is required in the situation, because someone is in need of this answer. Personalized thoughts that arise due to ego-centric desires cease and thoughts become impersonal.

With Self-stabilization, what happens is not change, but transformation. Change is just an alteration; transformation is a paradigm shift.

When you begin to climb the stairs of a roof-less house to reach the terrace, you move from the first step to the second. Though this is a change, you are still on the stairs. When you move from the second step to the third, you can probably get a better view of the house, but you remain on the stairs. Each step does improve your view of the house. You are able to get a relatively clearer view of the house, which was otherwise constrained by the pillars and beams. This is change.

But when you leave the stairs behind and step onto the terrace, it is a shift or transformation. Your view becomes totally unhindered. You can clearly see what part of the house was hidden from your view when you were downstairs. You are able to see the obstacles that were limiting your view downstairs. You are also able to effortlessly see what others who are downstairs are not able to see.

The key here is the instant shift of perspective that comes with reaching the terrace. In the context of life, this implies gaining a total view of the unseen.

With change, ignorance continues, because you still perceive from the level of the mind, through judgments, logical premise, assumptions and memory. However, with transformation, the entire structure of the programmed mind is transcended. You rise above mental perceptions (the stairs) and intuitively know from the Self (the terrace).

You get a clear view of Nature's way of working. With such clarity, there remains no question of doubt or distrust. There is complete faith in how life plays out; whatever happens, happens according to the Divine Plan. So much that one transcends the need to place faith or believe in something; because one knows!

When you can see, there is no need to believe

Let us understand this further with the help of an example.

Suppose that a rope is tied between two hilltops. People are asked whether they can walk the rope from one hilltop to the other. Most people would backout out of fear of falling. Even those, who have practiced and are skilled at rope-walking, may backout due to the perceived risk associated with scaling the rope between two hills.

A rare enthusiast, who has unshakeable belief in his skill and competence, the will to accomplish such a feat, and the hunger for such adventure may still attempt it and succeed.

But now here's the catch. What if the rope is *invisible*? Would anyone attempt it? Even if one was given 100% assurance that one cannot fall, one would not attempt walking on an *invisible* rope. Firstly, it seems irrational and foolish in logical terms to attempt such a feat. Secondly, one cannot get oneself to believe that it is possible. Thirdly, one will not have faith on the assurance that is being given.

And yet, there can be those rare ones, who can muster the courage to take the leap of faith, mainly because they place unquestionable and unflinching trust in the assurance that is being given.

Yes, this example may seem bizarre and farfetched, but in a way, it helps to consider the grandeur of the state that transcends faith.

For the one who has transcended faith, there is no question of believing in his skill or taking a leap of faith. This is because the rope that is invisible to others is *not* invisible to him! He *knows* it is there; he *sees* it, because he is on the terrace! He sees what others can't. Walking the 'invisible' rope is natural and effortless for him. He sees the unseen! He knows how life works.

How does this relate to our life?

When one transcends faith, life gets into alignment with the divine flow. In life situations, choices emerge from the unseen, without the need for careful thinking or deliberate effort. It happens naturally, with ease, because that is our true nature. We are ease-in-action. We are faith-in-action.

We do not need to think about our true nature; we just need to be our true nature. Thinking is needed for whatever is not our true nature. Questions like "How should I do this?" arise only in matters that are not our true nature. For example, "How should I live?", "How should I deal with this situation?", How should I make this decision?", "How can I get rid of sorrow?" As long as you get such thoughts, you are away from your true nature.

When you abide in your nature, such questions end. You will not need to know "how to". Every answer, every solution, will emerge from the Source spontaneously. Life becomes a divine song that radiates warmth and melody, touching others, inspiring them to raise their faith and transcend it!

APPENDIX 1
THE JOURNEY OF FAITH

The journey of faith traverses through seven kinds of faith, lending a strong unshakeable foundation to our lives. It is essential to cultivate these seven kinds of faith. Let us understand what these seven kinds are.

1. Faith in Ourselves

You may have heard that confidence wins you half the battle, there and then. If someone lacks confidence, they have lost half the battle even before they begin to fight!

Do not misunderstand *'having faith in ourselves'* as having faith in one's cerebral intelligence. While the intelligence of the brain has its uses, it also has its limitations. A person, who has too much faith in his intelligence, becomes arrogant and believes that only what he thinks in every situation is right. This brings stagnation to his intellect. An arrogant person refuses to learn and grow because he believes his intellect is far and above everything else.

Faith in oneself is *not* faith in one's intelligence. Faith in oneself is the faith in one's ability to persevere. It is having faith that not only can one succeed at something but can persevere in the face of challenges and setbacks. Such confidence in oneself helps one stand up to any challenge in life.

In addition to ourselves, we should also have trust in our relations. Relationship with one's parents, with one's spouse or partner, children, siblings, friends, employees, bosses, clients –all these relationships need to be based on the foundation of trust. Stronger the trust, the longer the relationship – it is a simple rule. Only trust can make relationships stronger. In the absence of it, it withers and dies.

It is also important to use the power of your own faith to give others the confidence they need. For example, some parents discourage their children from trying and experimenting new things. They often do things for their children themselves. While their intention behind doing this is to ensure their child's safety, they fail to understand that they are inadvertently hurting their confidence. The child's faith in oneself remains a bonsai. Parents need to have faith in their children's abilities and allow them to lead their own lives in their own way, so that they get a chance to explore and foster their inner qualities.

2. Faith on the Guru

> Swami Vivekananda was very close and dear to his Guru, Ramakrishna Paramhansa. After the Guru left his mortal body, there was a point in his life when Swami Vivekananda felt acutely lost. Try as he might, he could not find the right direction to take the next step.
>
> One fine day, while meditating, he prayed to his Guru for guidance. He continued to meditate for many hours, awaiting his Guru's reply. Finally, he saw an image of Ramakrishna Paramhansa walking on water towards the west. Swami Vivekananda deciphered this image as two messages: One, that he was to take a boat journey and that he was to head towards the western world. It was then that he came to know about the Parliament of Religions to be held in Chicago in the year 1893 and chose to attend and address it.

This incident illustrates that when a disciple has complete faith on his Guru, he always receives the right guidance from him. When such a disciple walks one step, his Guru walks ten, to help him out. Having unshakeable, unconditional and unquestioning faith on the Guru, transforms life itself into a miracle.

History has witnessed and shall continue to witness many such disciples whose lives inspire divine faith. Saint Meera, Saint Dnyaneshwar, Saint Kabir, Guru Angad... the list goes on. All these lives are an inspiration to the seekers of truth even today and for generations to come.

3. Faith on the Guru's Teachings

In addition to having faith on the Guru, a disciple needs to have faith on his teachings. Every word spoken by the Guru has the potential to help the disciple realize his ultimate goal. When the disciple understands this, he doesn't question the Guru's teachings and faithfully applies them in his life, however simple or illogical the teaching may seem to be.

There have been many saints, who continued to spread the teachings of their Guru to the masses, after their Guru passed away. This is possible, only when the disciple has deep faith on their Guru's teachings.

4. Faith on the Guru's Faith

Having faith on the Guru's faith may not make sense at first, but this is the most important kind of faith with regards to attaining the ultimate purpose of life. At the beginning of the spiritual journey, it is possible that a person may find it hard to believe that he will eventually attain Self-realization, but his Guru places complete faith and assurance despite all odds in the disciple's divine possibility. At such a stage in the journey when the disciple doesn't believe in himself, he has to place faith on the Guru's faith, that he can attain liberation.

5. Faith on God (Nature)

People believe in the existence of God, but that does not necessarily mean they have complete faith on Him. Based on the experiences and incidents that they come across in their lives, they keep re-evaluating their faith on God. Every time a wish is fulfilled, their faith grows and every time something undesirable happens, their faith diminishes. If they were to have complete and unflinching faith on God, they will be able to lead a much easier and effortless life. Le us understand this with the example of a married couple that was travelling in a boat.

> The sea was getting violent and the boat bobbed up and down. The wife was getting increasingly frightened at the thought of drowning. The husband, on the other hand, was sitting, quite calm and composed. The wife was surprised at the stillness of her husband in the face of such a dangerous situation.
>
> "How are you not afraid?" she exclaimed over the sounds of gushing waves.
>
> In reply, the husband extracted a sharp pocket knife, placed the blade of the knife on her neck, and said, "Are you not afraid that I might harm you with this knife?"
>
> "Why, no!" she said, "I know you love me and wouldn't even think of hurting me!"
>
> "You're right," the husband replied, keeping the knife away. "I do love you, and so does God love us all. Just the way you have faith that I will never hurt you, I have complete faith on God that he would never wish us any harm. It is owing to this faith that I am calm."

Having complete faith on God helps us lead a calm, easy and effortless life. When a father tosses a child up in the air, the child has unquestionable faith on him that he shall keep him from falling. Owing to this faith, the child is able to enjoy the situation instead of getting restless and terrified. Such is the faith we need to have on God.

6. Faith on God's Faith

God's faith on us humans says that, "Self-realization is your birthright," but few are able to believe in it. Even fewer make it to the ultimate goal of life to attain Self-realization and complete the journey.

Even though their words may differ every religious scripture speaks about this state of Self-realization. But most people tend to neglect this wisdom, passing it off as bookish knowledge that they feel is irrelevant to practical living. And most people lead a life of insecurity, despair, guilt and disharmony.

When we learn about God's faith on us, we open ourselves to a new perspective of life. It opens up doors to unimaginable infinite potential, and so begins a magical journey.

7. Faith in God's Will

We have heard the words, "Neither winds may blow, nor leaves may stir, but for the will of God." Whatever happens, happens by His will. It is imperative for us to have faith in God's will.

We hear people blame God for the hardships that they suffer. Those affected by accidents, famines, floods, epidemics and other hazards, complain to God saying, "I've never wished anyone harm; why this injustice then? What have I done wrong to be meted out such a fate?" The pain and suffering that these questions arise from are understandable, but we need to have faith in God's will and understand His ways.

We forget that whatever happens to us is firstly a direct result of our own deliberate or inadvertent prayers. Secondly, the incident has come to teach us something and make us stronger. Every seemingly negative incident – without exception – has a positive purpose behind it. It is just that the positive purpose may not always be obvious. It is hence necessary to believe in the unseen by having faith in God's will.

In the face of every untoward incident and negative experience, let us express our faith in God's will by saying, "Thy will is my will" and then experience the magic of life that follows. When our faith remains unmoved, situations move on, we remain untouched!

APPENDIX 2
FAITH, HOPE AND CONFIDENCE

(*This chapter is a collection of answers by Sirshree to questions by seekers of Truth on the subject of Faith, Hope and Confidence.*)

Question: If faith is indeed such a profound and powerful force, why don't people experience it in daily life?

Answer: Faith is undoubtedly the most profound force in the universe. However, to be able to unleash its true potential, one needs to know the principles that faith works on. We need to understand the ways of Nature and the laws that govern them.

Man has also lost the quality of giving. His logic says that by giving away, he will lose. It has to be learned that whatever one gives away, returns manifold. Happiness magnifies when shared. There is not a single person in this world who has absolutely nothing to offer to others. If nothing, one can at least offer his time and effort; he can help others work through their troubles; he can wipe someone's tears; he can share his knowledge; he can bring a smile to someone. It does not matter *what* or *how much* you give, as long as you give something. Those who give, have experienced how it all comes back in multiples.

The logic of the so-called practical world makes people behave contrary to this. People want to receive before they give. Because they don't give, they don't receive and because they don't receive they have all the more reason to not give! This tendency itself is the hurdle in realizing one's true potential.

"I will wish someone on their birthday only if they have wished me on mine. I will gift them the equivalent of what they gifted me. I will give others attention only if they give it to me." Such is the limited and frivolous thinking people are reduced to today. It is time to realize the importance of the unseen laws of Nature so that we may experience the power of faith in our daily lives.

Question: Is there such a thing as 'too much or excessive faith'? Is it the same as 'overconfidence'?

Answer: Consider the example of an intelligent student, who usually scores excellent marks, but fails his final exams. People usually make remarks that he failed due to his *overconfidence*. The fact is that there is no such thing as overconfidence. The word, although coined and used extensively, actually does not exist. Overconfidence is in reality carelessness and ignorance. The student did not fail because he had too much confidence; he failed because he was careless. He did not care to study as hard as he did at other times.

Just as there is no such thing as too much confidence, there is no such thing as too much faith either. On the contrary, even the greatest amount of faith one can have is still not enough, because faith is infinite. It cannot be limited.

Let us understand the true meaning of overconfidence with the help of a story:

Three disciples were taking an evening stroll through the market when they suddenly saw a elephant running wild in their direction, crushing whatever came in his way, uprooting plants and shrubs with his trunk. The mahout, sitting atop the elephant, was yelling out to people, asking them to get out of the way.

Hearing the mahout's words, two of the disciples quickly ran to safety, but the third disciple stood where he was. The other two disciples urged him to join them at the safe spot but he refused to budge. "Our Guru has taught us," he said to his fellow disciples, "that God rushes to help those in need and protects his devotees."

Soon, the elephant reached where the disciple stood and with one big swoop of his trunk, swept the disciple away. The disciple was flung and crashed against a large tree, falling down, badly wounded and bruised. The two disciples looked on with horror and as soon as the elephant had passed, rushed to the aid of their friend.

Later when they were at the hermitage, they recounted the whole incident to their Guru and asked him, "O great one, what the disciple said wasn't untrue. You did teach us that God always protects his disciples, come what may. Then how did he get hurt? Why didn't God protect him?"

The Guru calmly replied, "God did try to protect him. Not just him, but you two as well and everyone else on that street. He did that through the mahout, who was warning everyone to make sure they got out of the way. You and everybody else on the street heeded his words and ran to your safety, but he ignored God's words. He carelessly and foolishly stood in the way of the elephant and paid the price!"

Would you say that the third disciple had 'too much faith'? Was he overconfident? No! He was ignorant and careless!

Question: By vesting all our faith on the Guru, are we not losing our own confidence?

Answer: If one has complete faith on the Guru, it does not mean one should not have faith in oneself. This is like saying if you have faith in yourself, you should not have faith in your parents, friends, spouse or anybody else.

On the contrary, it is the Guru who teaches us what it is to have complete faith in ourselves. It is *because* we aren't able to have faith in ourselves, that we have to have faith in the Guru, so that He may teach us how to believe in ourselves. And once we are able to believe in ourselves, it doesn't mean we do not have faith in our Guru anymore.

The limited logic of the mind says that all our faith can only be vested in one place – *either* in ourselves *or* on the Guru. If all the faith is vested on the Guru, there is none left for oneself, and if all of it is vested in oneself, none is left for the Guru. This is far from the truth.

Faith is not like some cargo, about which it can be said that if it is present there, then it is not here and if it is brought here, it is not present there! The Guru is the bridge between the disciple and God. He teaches us to have faith in our true Self. As we mature, we gradually realize that having faith in ourselves and having faith in the Guru are one and the same thing. The more we get to know our true Self, the clearer the oneness of it all becomes. We realize that Guru, God, Grace, Faith and ourselves – are all one!

Question: It is said that numerology, astrology, Fengshui, *Vastushastra*, tarot cards, all have scientific basis. There are numerous examples of how people wear rings and talismans that fulfil their wishes and bring them success. Do all these things really work and how?

Answer: People usually only know half the truth about these things due to which they give way to superstitions and blind beliefs. It is hence, very important to understand these concepts deeply and thoroughly.

Nature has made a number of natural things available to humans that help his mental and physical wellbeing. Just as there are medicinal herbs, plants and flowers for physical wellbeing, there are also certain stones and metals that protect us from negative vibrations, to a certain extent. Some stones are known to emit vibrations that calm the mind and bring peace to the bearer.

But there is a missing link in the understanding about how these things work. While rings and talismans do affect us, the effect is limited. However, the moment people wear them, it brings about a great shift in their self-belief. Whether it is a ring, a talisman, a necklace, a bracelet, a stone or some elaborate ritual – the moment a person comes into contact with it, his faith changes. He thinks, "Now that I am wearing this ring, my success is guaranteed!", "Now that I have the talisman around my neck, I am completely safe!" This faith works in their life.

The artifacts foster a positive feeling and the wearer begins to radiate a positive vibe. Positive vibes attract more positive vibes and the person sees a flow of positivity in his life. Positive ideas, positive people, positive situations – everything that is conducive to the fulfilment of the person's wishes begins to flow towards him. The positivity frees the person of all his fears, doubts and insecurities, and consequently his wishes begin to manifest.

But the person forgets that it was not the artifacts that brought about the manifestation of his wishes – it was the change in his thoughts, his belief system, his level of faith. The artifacts only triggered the change.

As the person experiences the manifestation of his wishes, his faith grows stronger. Faith influences feelings, feelings influence actions, actions influence the outcome and the outcome reinforces the faith to complete the faith frame. These artifacts only help initiate the faith frame in the person's life, however once the faith has been awakened, they are not needed. They have done their job and can be discarded.

However, we see that they become crutches that people hold on to for all their life, assigning them the credit for their peace, happiness and success, instead of the real force that worked for them.

Question: Should we then not believe in numerology, astrology at all and instead focus on giving direction to our thoughts and cultivating faith?

Answer: Absolutely! It is not being said that numerology, astrology and other such fields are entirely useless. They do have a certain credibility, but is it is limited. These can only be helpful to people who have lost all hope in life or have completely lost faith in the face of constant adversity and have become depressed.

As stated by the field of astrology, the stars and planets do affect the state of our mind. The moon affects the tides on earth. Our body largely constitutes water. 90% of the human body weight comes from water. If the moon can affect such large bodies of water as the seas and oceans, it certainly affects the human body.

Keeping in mind such facts, our ancestors studied and developed the concepts of astrology, horoscope and zodiac signs. The purpose of these studies was only to make people aware of their possibilities, so as to help them be prepared. The scholars who studied these fields knew this very well. They knew that the predictions made by astrology and numerology were not to be considered as the absolute truth and the delimiting line of one's potential. They are only to be taken as guidelines.

Consider a person who goes to a doctor to get some medical tests done. After examining the test results, the doctor tells the patient that there is a chance that he might have diabetes in the future. The patient feels dejected, thinking he is definitely going to have diabetes in his future. However, that is not what the doctor wanted to convey. He only expressed the *possibility* of diabetes. Ideally the person should thank the doctor for highlighting the possibility and take all the preventive care against diabetes.

Similarly, understand that astrology and numerology also indicate certain possibilities. And there are unlimited possibilities waiting to manifest in the unseen! One should not consider what an astrologer or numerologist tells us as the final and absolute reality. Nothing but faith has the ultimate power to influence our lives and manifest our wishes.

Question: What is hope and how is it related to faith?

Answer: Hope is the tiny ray of light that tears through the darkness of negativity. When a person is surrounded by negativity, hope is what gives him the inspiration to keep going. Hope gives the person the strength to persevere in the face of adversity. Hope is deeply related to faith. When a person finds it difficult to have faith that he can succeed at something, he begins with the hope to succeed. Hope paves the way for faith.

APPENDIX 3
PRINCIPLES OF FAITH – QUICK REFERENCE

Principle 1

As your Faith, so your Feelings. As your Feelings, so your Actions. As your Actions, so the Results. As the Results, so your Faith.

Principle 2

First sow the seed of faith, then comes its fruit. Better the seed of faith, better its fruit.

Principle 3

Life is on autopilot. Trust it. Nature is always serving up your highest good.

Principle 4

When we consciously express the *Faith of God* in words, it brings us into alignment with our divine nature and unfolds our highest potential.

Principle 5

Betrayal is a myth. Faith is the truth.

Principle 6

Inner transformation is brought about with 100% faith.

Principle 7

Everything in Nature is automatically progressing towards its state of ultimate evolution. When faith evolves into its utmost state, it becomes Divine Faith.

■■■

You can mail your opinion or feedback on this book to: books.feedback@tejgyan.org

About Sirshree

Sirshree's spiritual quest, which began during his childhood, led him on a journey through various schools of philosophy and meditation practices. He studied a wide range of literature on mind science and spirituality. After a long period of deep contemplation on the truth of life, his quest culminated in attaining the ultimate truth.

Sirshree espouses, "All spiritual paths that lead to the truth begin differently but culminate at the same point – Understanding. This understanding is complete in itself. Listening to this understanding is enough to attain the Truth." Over the last two decades, he has dedicated his life to raise mass consciousness.

Sirshree has delivered more than 4000 discourses that throw light on this understanding. He has designed a system for wisdom, which makes it accessible to all. This system has inspired people from all walks of life to progress on their journey of the Truth. Thousands of seekers join in a virtual prayer for World Peace and Global Healing daily at 9:09 am and 9:09 pm.

About Tej Gyan Foundation

Tej Gyan Foundation is a non-profit organization founded on the teachings of Sirshree. The Foundation disseminates Tejgyan – the wisdom that guides one from self-development to Self-realization, leading towards Self-stabilization.

The Foundation's system for imparting wisdom has been assessed by international quality auditors and accredited with the ISO 9001:2015 certification. This wisdom has been presented in a simple, systematic, and practically applicable form that makes it accessible to people from all walks of life, regardless of religion, caste, social strata, country, or belief system.

The Foundation has centers in more than 400 cities and towns across India and other countries. The mission of Tej Gyan Foundation is to create a highly evolved society by leading seekers from negative thoughts to positive thoughts and further, from positive thoughts to Happy thoughts. A 'Happy thought' is the auspicious thought of being free from all thoughts, leading to the state of supreme bliss beyond thoughts.

If you seek such wisdom that leads you beyond mere knowledge, dissolves all problems, frees you from all limiting beliefs, reveals the true nature of divinity, and establishes you in the ultimate truth, then it is time to discover Tejgyan; it is time to rise above the mundane knowledge of words and experience Tejgyan!

The MahaAasmani Magic of Awakening Retreat

Self-development to Self-realization towards Self-stabilization

Do you wish to experience unconditional happiness that is not dependent on any reason? Happiness that is permanent and only increases with time? Do you wish to experience love, peace, self-belief, harmony in relationships, prosperity, and true contentment? Do you wish to progress in all facets of your life, viz. physical, mental, social, financial, and spiritual?

If you seek answers to these questions and are thirsty for the ultimate truth, then you are welcome to participate in the MahaAasmani Magic of Awakening retreat organized by Tej Gyan Foundation. This is the Foundation's flagship retreat based on the teachings of Sirshree.

The purpose of this retreat

The purpose of this retreat is that every human being should:

- Discover the answer to "Who am I" and "Why am I?" through direct experience and be established in ultimate bliss.

- Learn the art of living in the present, free from the burden of the past and the anxiety of the future.

- Acquire practical tools to help quieten the chattering mind and dissolve problems.

- Discover missing links in the practices of Meditation (*Dhyana*), Action (*Karma*), Wisdom (*Gyana*), and Devotion (*Bhakti*).

About Books by Sirshree

Sirshree's published work includes more than 150 book titles, some of which have been translated into more than 10 languages. His literature provides a profound reading on various topics of practical living and unravels the missing links in karma, wisdom, devotion, meditation, and consciousness.

His books have been published by leading publishing houses like Penguin, Hay House, Bloomsbury, Wisdom Tree, Jaico, etc. "The Source" book series, authored by Sirshree, has sold over 10 million copies. Various luminaries and celebrities like His Holiness the Dalai Lama, publishers Mr. Reid Tracy, Ms. Tami Simon and Yoga Master Dr. B. K. S. Iyengar have released Sirshree's books and lauded his work.

The Source
Attain Both, Inner Peace and Worldly success

Awaken the Power of Faith
Discover the 7 Principles of the Highest Power of the Universe

To order books authored by Sirshree, login to:
www.gethappythoughts.org
For further details, call: +91 9011013210

SELECT BOOKS AUTHORED BY SIRSHREE

   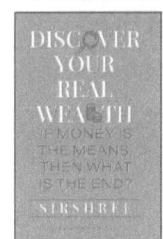

To order these and other books authored by Sirshree
Visit **www.gethappythoughts.org**

Tej Gyan Foundation – Contact details

Registered Office:
Happy Thoughts Building, Vikrant Complex, Near Tapovan Mandir, Pimpri, Pune 411017, INDIA. Contact: +91 20-27411240, +91 20-27412576

MaNaN Ashram:
Survey No. 43, Sanas Nagar, Nandoshi Gaon, Kirkatwadi Phata, Off Sinhagad Road, Taluka Haveli, Pune district - 411024, INDIA. Contact: +91 992100 8060.

WORLD PEACE PRAYER

Divine Light of Love, Bliss, and Peace is Showering;

The Golden Light of Higher Consciousness is Rising;

All negativity on Earth is Dissolving;

Everyone is in Peace and Blissfully Shining;

O God, Gratitude for Everything!

Members of Tej Gyan Foundation have been offering this impersonal mass prayer for many years. Those who are happy can offer this prayer. Those feeling low or suffering from illness can receive healing with this prayer.

If you are feeling troubled or sick, please sit to receive the healing effect of this prayer. Visualize that the divine white healing light is being showered on earth through the prayers of thousands and is also reaching you, bringing you peace and good health. You can dwell in this feeling for some time and then offer your gratitude to those offering the prayer.

A Humble Appeal

More than a million peace lovers pray for World Peace and Global Healing every morning and evening at 9:09. Also, a prayer (in Hindi) to elevate consciousness is webcast every day on YouTube at 3:30 pm and 9:00 pm IST. Please participate in this noble endeavor.

www.ingramcontent.com/pod-product-compliance
Lightning Source LLC
LaVergne TN
LVHW041949070526
838199LV00051BA/2957